DIPLOMATIC ARCHITECTURE OF
AFRICAN UNION

Thaddeus Mbalian Esq.

Published in Nigeria

ISBN: 978-978-53646-0-6

Foreword

Diplomatic Architecture of African Union is written by **Thaddeus Aondongu Mbalian,** a Private Legal Practitioner in the Law firm of Noble Crest Solicitors based in Abuja, Nigeria.

The core argument advanced in the book, which appears to be the central idea and the driving force that has stimulated the publication of the book is the global competition for supremacy in various dimensions among the nations of the world.

All Nations of the world are in a global competitive race for supremacy in various dimensions of human endeavour, be it military supremacy, economic might, viable political system or otherwise. Africa as a continent with a conglomeration of countries is not left out in the race. The author argues that, for over a number of decades, the African Continent has been struggling to be recognized by the global community as a force to reckon with.

Daunting development challenges, have however, negated the efforts of African Nations towards attaining these expectations. There was much hope, enthusiasm and expectations from the people of Africa, that with political independence, economic development would be realized with Africans taking full charge of their destinies. The situation, just a few years into independence of most African countries, revealed that, with retrospection, much of the optimism and expectations had been misplaced and that the leadership and the people had not really taken stock of what the task of administering the new states entailed.

Consequently, there was need to create a forum where Africans would discuss and freely express their views on global issues. This gave rise to the formation of the Organization of African Union (OAU). The OAU had noble ideals reflecting the wind of change blowing across the Continent, promoting political and economic betterment of the Africa and its people, combating colonialism and defending the sovereignty of African states. The author argues that with the transformation of OAU into AU with the sole aim of providing a platform for Africans and their grassroots organizations to be more involved in discussions and decision making on the problems and challenges facing the African continent, Africa seemed set on a solid pathway to progress, and for a while it seemed as if that sense of optimism was justified.

Very clearly, the AU has a mandate and clearly defined objectives. The book, **the Diplomatic Architecture of African Union** is an attempt to lay bare the issues and reasons behind the formation of the regional body. The book attempts to discuss the successes and failures of the Organization. Suggestions have been made as the way forward for what the author calls "betterment of Africans".

The book is timely written. There is urgent need to foster development in order to justify the truly independent status of the African Continent. The themes covered in the book are of intrinsic relevance to the understanding of the issues relating to making the Regional Body functional and effective.

The ten- chapter book captures the topics relating to the concept of international institutions, tracing the historic emergence of such institutions and the legal framework guiding their operations.

Chapter Three of the book focuses on the Organization of African Unity (OAU) with an in depth discussion on its objectives and major organs. The formation of common economic policy has been treated in Chapter Four with a detailed discussion on the New Partnership for Africa's Development (NEPAD).

Also covered in the book is the legal effects of the activities of the AU, highlighting the intervention by AU in support of constitutional Governments across Africa. The Author has equally discussed Social effects of the activities of the AU. In an attempt to draw comparison with other international organizations, the author has given an in depth discussion of European Union (EU) as a model for Regional Organizations.

Furthermore, the book discusses inherent challenges facing AU. One of such challenges confronting the continent as discussed in one of the chapters is the spate of conflicts within member states arising from political and economic mismanagement and the various measures being adopted by the Union to restore stability. The book has suggested the way forward for the Union. Interestingly, the book has a dedicated appendix which the author calls the Constitutive Act of the African Union. The appendix has provided very useful information about the instrument guiding the operations of AU.

In view of the intellectual relevance and the quality discussions in this book, I find the book quite appropriate for use by Diplomats, Students of History of Diplomatic Studies and Political Science. Equally, the book is useful to the Political Class as well as legal profession.

Professor Nicholas Akise Ada MSTAN
Professor of Science Education
Former Honourable Minister of State 1, Foreign Affairs
Ministry of Foreign Affairs
Federal Republic of Nigeria

Dedication

This book is dedicated to all lovers and upholders of the black race.

Acknowledgement

remain eternally grateful to God Almighty who provided me the inspiration and good health from the beginning to the end of putting my thoughts together. Words are not enough to express my profound gratitude to the following people who have in one way or the other assisted me through the various stages of accomplishing my dream. I beseech God to reward them abundantly for their commitment to the project, either in terms of material inputs, moral advice and other contributions to the work. They are: Mallam Musa Abdulazez Adaba of **Summit Associates** who made series of inputs to the work, as well as shouldered the responsibility of publishing the book. Professor Nicholas Akise Adah, former Minister of State, Foreign Affairs, for providing an incisive foreword; Your Honourable, I remain ever appreciative. Others are: Dr.(Mrs) M.M. Dura, Special Adviser to the Governor of Benue State on NEPAD & MDGs, my mother, Anna Mbalian, Rev. & Mrs Hough, Dennis Mbalian, my wife, Nancy Mbalian, our wonderful children, Secivir, Sena and Pineter Caleb Mbalian who lent me their precious time to put this work together. My colleagues in the office; Wilson Iorshe Esq, Isaac Vembe Esq, S.A. Chinngiga Esq, our former corper, Fortune Orji, among others. Mr. Aloo's contributions are equally acknowledged.

I beg the forgiveness of all those who have been with me over the course of the years and whose names I have failed to mention. Thanks and may God bless you.

Table of Contents

CHAPTER ONE

Introduction

he importance attached to possible solutions to the challenges of development in the area of political, economic and social stability in the continent of Africa necessitated the burning desire to embark on this noble work. The Book **DIPLOMATIC ARCHITECTURE OF AFRICAN UNION,** therefore is set to examine the various frameworks put in place by African leaders to address such developmental issues as well as to make recommendations. The framework ranges from legal, economic and institutional measures that have survived from one generation to another. For decades, series of initiatives have come up from various member states all targeting at how best to move the continent forward in the quest to join the comity of global community. It is important to remind ourselves that the name of the continental body had changed in the effort to salvage the situation, but the situation seems to remain the same. What is responsible for the state of inertia? Lack of political will among the member states, or absence of visionary leadership? Readers might actually ask, what is in a name? It is the fervent belief that the book will be of immense help to many scholars, legal practitioners, diplomats, students and policy makers alike in our collective search for harmonious and mutual co-existence in the African continent.

The need for peaceful co-existence and a defined way of human interaction at the global sphere called for fora under which issues of common global interest were and still are to be discussed. The idea started like a mustard seed and received accolades, though not without systematic hitches. Historically, the development of international institution could be traced from the increase and growing number of independent and sovereign geo-political units of the world. The conference system was developed but due to its frail nature, the initiators desired a more stable and stronger system which could serve futuristic purposes. The dream which materialised through formation of some inter-state organisations later gave birth to a globally known organisation called the League of Nations which came into being after the First World War. Though short-lived, it metamorphosed into the current United Nations Organisation, whose charter was provided for formation of, or recognised regional organisations such as the African Union. [1]

The African Union is a successor to the Organisation of African Unity (OAU), the intergovernmental organisation for African states in existence since 1963, created with the aim of strengthening integration among member states, and the voice of African continent in global affairs. With the end of the Cold War, the final liberation of Africa and the reshaping of international political scene, African Heads of States recognised that the Organisation of African Unity (hereinafter called OAU) framework was not adequate to meet the needs for greater intercontinental policy co-ordination and stronger economic growth, and that a greater commitment to democratic government at national level was necessary to strengthen Africa's own voice on the international stage. Then the stage was set for the introduction of a new born baby, African Union, "the Messiah of the continent". The envisaged new body was to be structured after the European Union's institutional framework.

---

1   See Article 52(1) of the United Nations Charter.

The constitutive Act of the African Union, its founding document, was adopted by the Heads of States in Lome, Togo, and entered into force in 2001. The Union, however, took off officially in July, 2002 with its inaugural meeting held in Durban, South Africa. The Union has 53 member States; only Morocco that is not a member among the States on the Continent because it withdrew from the then OAU in 1984 to protest the admission of Saharawi Arab Democratic Republic (Western Sahara) as a member of the Organisation.

African Union has embedded African Economic Community, which was established by a treaty adopted in Abuja, Nigeria, in 1991 and became part of its predecessor, as part of its system. The constitutive Act of the Union and the Treaty of African Economic Community are said to be complementary, and jointly provide the legal basis for continental integration. Most of the key organs of the Union are established under its constitutive Act, but some are set under Protocols to the constitutive Act or the Abuja Treaty establishing the African Economic Community, free-standing treaties or other legal documentation. Both the constitutive Act and the Abuja Treaty are said to be capable of putting African continent on the pedestal of globalisation, and indeed the needed development.

This book looks at the African Union as a continental organisation whose aim is to promote peaceful co-existence among member-States. It will x-ray the Union's performance since inception and where necessary, proffer some suggestions.

The basis for the formation of the Union

In the second half of the 20th Century, particularly in the 1960s, African States witnessed a turn-around as most of the States gained their independence. The need for self-determination by the African States paved way for at least political independence and after the attainment of independence, the challenge of how to strengthen the self-determination and the united spirit of the States prior to independence became a concern by the new African leaders.[2] The spirit then culminated in the confederal arrangement which was consecrated at Addis Ababa in Ethiopia thus the charter of the Organisation of African Unity emerged. Principally, the organisation of African Unity (hereinafter referred to as the Organisation) was inter alia, to promote unity and the solidarity of African States. The organisation through its various organs or institutions tried to achieve its aims and objectives but could not achieve all, and therefore, it became necessary to fashion out an institution which could deliver the set goals for the growth, development and progress of the African continent, considering the emerging social, political and economic realities in Africa and the whole world. African Union (hereinafter called the Union) emerged as a successor to the Organisation of African Unity in July, 2002.[3] One of the noble objectives that the book seeks to achieve is to examine the new Union which is believed to be the "saviour" of the African continent.

In embarking on the voyage (of discovery) herein, the following fundamental posers will be considered: (1) what really prompted the change from Organisation of African Unity to the new African Union? And what is the fundamental difference between Organisation of African Unity and African Union? (2) To what extent has the Union achieved the set objectives within its few years of existence? If not what are the measures put in place

---

2   Sands P. and Klein P. (ed) Bowett's Law of International Institutions (London: Sweet & Maxwell, 2001) p.244

3   "Transition from the OAU to African Union" http://www.au2002.gov.za/docs/background/oau-to-auhtm visited 7/7/2010 being a document for transition at OAU headquarters.

to ensure the realisation or improvement on the journey so far? (3) Are the member states committed to the realisation of the basic objectives of the union?

Definition of Terms

In order to engender a better understanding or grasp of the issues involved herein, it is pertinent to explain and or define certain basic concepts that constitute technical terms... Consequently, concepts such as Union, international institution and State will be dealt with hereunder. The first concept worthy of consideration is "Union." It refers to "when two or more things that have joined together to become one thing; used especially for countries or organisations that have been formed in this way."[4] This definition though sound, it may be faulted in one breath. The emphasis placed on things in the first part of the definition renders it defective. This is because human beings who form unions or bring things together to form a union are completely left out of the definition, thereby making it incomplete. Be that as it may, the concept Union can be considered to mean the coming together of persons, things, countries or organisations with a view to achieving certain goals. This could be done based on the contractual or mutual agreement of the parties thereto.

The next concept to be considered is "international institution" which is the bedrock of the discourse in this noble work. The term international institution otherwise referred to as international organisation has no universally accepted definition. However, attempts have been made by scholars to fashion definitions to the concept. The issue of definition of topical concept(s) is an epidemic that plagues every field of endeavour

---

4   Sinclair J. (ed) BBC English Dictionary (London: BBC English and Harper Collins Publishers, 1992) p.1283

as several attempts are made but without wider or global acceptability. Statutorily, the Vienna Convention on the Law of Treaties between States and International Organisations (1986) takes a minimalist approach on the definition of the concept as follows: "International Organisation means an Intergovernmental Organisation."[5] This definition lacks universal acceptability because it fails to recognise the fact that not only inter-governmental organisations that are called international organisations, or institutions. Private or non-governmental associations such as Red Cross Society, Boys Brigade, Girls Brigade as well as some human rights associations also have global geographical widespread and international status. Therefore, to make a sweeping assertion that international organisation is an inter-governmental organisation fails short of a good definition.

Another scholar considered the concept of international institution to mean "an entity which has been set up by means of a treaty concluded by states to engage in cooperation in a particular field and which has its own organs."[6] As sound as this definition may appear to be, it fall victim of criticisms. In the first place, it appears to be focussing only on "States" as only entities capable of forming international institutions thereby neglecting the private institutions which also have international recognition with distinct legal personality. Again, this is narrow in scope because it regards international institution as an entity that engages in "cooperation in a particular field." This assertion is far from being wholly true because many international institutions such as United Nations Organisation, African Union, among others are multi-disciplinary or multi-purpose

---

5   See Article 2 of the Vienna Convention on Law of Treaties between States and International Organisations, 1986
6   Reuter P (ed) Institutions et Relations International 3rd edn. (New Delhi: Institution Press, 1986) p.215

institutions. In as much as there are specialised international institutions, it does not mean that it is a general trend in international institutional sphere.

Some commentators have argued that, for an association or entity to qualify to be regarded as an international institution, it must have the following qualities:

(a) Its membership must be composed of states and/or other international organisations;

(b) It must be established by a treaty;

(c) It must have an autonomous will distinct from that of its members and be vested with legal personality; and

(d) It must be capable of adopting norms addressed to its members.[7]

The above definition suffers some loopholes even though it is wider in scope. The first defect emanating from the definition is the laying of emphasis on states and/or international organisations as the only entities that form an international institution. It forgets the fact that international institutions such as International Law Association (1873) (now International Bar Association), International Literary and Artistic Association, etc. are organizations formed by private individuals. Apart from that, the definition places much emphasis on treaty as the only instrument with which an international institution can be formed. This again renders it defective because some international institutions' status and activities are regulated by national laws. [8]Flowing from the above therefore, it is quite clear that the above definition does not apply in all folds to the concept, "international institution."

Having critically considered various attempts made by statute and scholars to explain or define the concept, it is ap-

7   Sands P. and Klein P. (ed) op cit p.16
8   Ibid

posite to provide a functional definition for the concept. Thus, international institution could best be defined as an autonomous body or entity set up by or governed by a constituent instrument and/or other laws, which expresses its independence through common organs and has capacity to act on the international sphere.

Last but not the least to be considered is the term "State". According to Black's Law Dictionary,[9] State is "the political system of a body of people who are politically organised; the system of rules by which jurisdiction and authority are exercised over such a body of people." This definition is infested with a very fundamental defect in that it fails to recognise that the State does not operate in a vacuum, that is, it must operate within a given geographical entity. The use of the word "jurisdiction" in the definition could be inferred to mean judicial jurisdiction. The context in which it is used does not in any way refer to the territorial jurisdiction. Another salient defect garnered from the definition is its failure to include performance as an important characteristic of a State. Once a State comes into being, it is expected to remain in perpetuity.

Some scholars and jurists have also made attempts to define the concept of State. One of them is Salmond who defines state as follows: "a State or political society is an association of human beings established for the attainment of certain ends by certain means."[10] With respect to the learned scholar, this definition is fundamentally defective and it cannot stand the test of time. It omits salient features such as permanence, territory and governmental machinery through which certain ends are

---

9   Garner B.A. (ed) Black's Law Dictionary 8th edn (USA: West Publishing Co., 2004) p.1443
10   Salmond J. Jurisprudence edited by William G.L. 10th edn (London: Sweet & Maxwell, 1947) p.129

attained. Briefly on his part considered State to be "an institution that is to say, it is a system of relations which men establish among themselves as a means of securing certain objects, of which the most fundamental is system of order within which their activities can be carried on."[11] A careful look at the above definition reveals that it has some shortcomings. Some of the invaluable components of a State which are found wanting in the definition are permanence and geographical entity. Without a defined geographical entity, the State cannot operate; also the State is not created for a given period; it is meant to be permanent baring any unforseeability.

The definition of the State provided by Woolsey is however, considered to be widely acceptable. He defines it as follows "A State is a community of persons living within a certain limits of territory, under a permanent organisation which aims to secure prevalence of justice by self-imposed law. The organ of the State by which it relates with which other States are managed is government."[12] This definition therefore, is hereby adopted for this book as its own.

Objectives of the Book

The attainment of independence by most African countries in the 1960s indeed marked a turning point in the history of the continent hence (there was) the need for the young countries or states to have a common forum wherein fundamental issues affecting African continent would be discussed. This informed the idea behind the formation of Organisation of African Unity which fostered the unity of member States. Nevertheless, with the dawn of the new millennium with its attendant chal-

---

11   Brierly J.L. The Law of Nations 5th edn (London: Jonas Publishers, 1955) p.118
12   Woosley T.D. Introduction to the Study of International Law 5th edn (London: Jones Publishers, 1878) p.34

lenges, the member States (most of them) decided that Africa should have a forum that could effectively tackle the challenges of the new millennium. Thus, in July 2000, at Lome, Togo, the 53-member States adopted a constitutive Act of the formation of the Union which became operational in 2002.

This book aims at critically assessing the reasons for the transformation of the former organisation into the new Union which is believed to be the solution to Africa's emerging problems.

In addition to the above, the book concisely present to the readers the aims and objectives of the Union vis-à-vis the principles guiding operation. This will in a way help the would-be readers of the book in analysing the performance of the Union within its few years of existence. Another objective of the book is to equip the readers in examining the effects (if any) of the Union's activities on member-States, that is to say, whether the activities of the Union are in tandem with its charter. If they are, then to what extent have the activities created positive impacts on the citizenry of the member-States.

Apart from that, the research would evaluate the response of the member-States to the calls of the Union, particularly in relation to legal orders of the Union as well as other commitments. In either way, the users of the book whether from the academia, corporate body or policy makers, will be well positioned to understand the overall framework of the Union The book has provide an insight into the workings of the Union's mechanism and the socio-legal effects on the members therein.

What the book seeks to achieve

The essence of every publication is to explore avenues available to arrive at a particular position that will be of great value to the author and the public or other end users of the work in a given area. That being the case, the scope of this book, **Diplomatic Architecture of African Union** which is substantially part of my research works in the University, will be territorially and substantively based. Territorially, the book's research cover the entire African continent but with specific attention being paid to the African Union member-States who have been affected in one way or the other by the Union's performance since its inception. Substantively, this research is limited to international institutional law with particular consideration to the constitutive Act of African Union and other allied laws. The book clearly x-rays the laws and other frame work relating to or guiding the Union and its institutions as affecting the citizenry.

CHAPTER TWO

The Concept of International Institution

Introduction

The evolution of the modern nation-States and consequent development of an international order founded upon a growing number of independent and sovereign territorial units inevitably gave rise to questions of international co-existence.[13] For effective and efficient handling of issues which begged for the unified efforts of the sovereign nation-States, it became necessary to form associations under which those issues would be considered. The necessity therefore, propelled the formation of different international societies otherwise called international institutions.

Historical Emergence of International Institutions

The quest for international co-operation became inevitable as the independent units of the world were becoming most conscious of the inter-dependent nature of humanity. To this end, diplomatic representation became more widespread as the system expanded, and economic and political relations multiplied. However, it soon became apparent that diplomatic contacts in themselves were unable to cope completely with the complexities of the international system and the concept of international conference system evolved as a form of extended di-

---

13   Shaw M.N. International Law, 4th edn (Cambridge: Cambridge University Press, 1977) p.887

plomacy.[14] Some scholars have posited that development of international institutions has been, in the main, a response to the evident need arising from international intercourse rather than to the philosophical or ideological government.[15] The growth of international intercourse in the sense of the development of the relations between different actors – both private and public, natural and legal has been a constant feature of maturing societies; advances in the mechanics of transportation and communications combined with the desire for trade and commerce have produced a degree of intercourse which ultimately called for international regulation by international means.[16] The evolution of the consular system was to protect and promote the commercial activities of a State in a foreign port while ambassadorial system was evolved to promote political co-operation among nation-States; this system survives till date.

Nevertheless, situations soon arose in which the essentially bilateral relationship established by diplomatic embassies or missions proved inadequate. This is because some problems would arise wherein not only states which had diplomatic relations were involved, but three or more states would also be concerned. Then the idea of institutional conference emerged whereby as many States as were involved in that problem were represented.[17] The conference system dealt with problems that concerned more than two or three States and in many cases resulted in an international treaty or formal pact. The first major instance of this occurred with the Peace of Westphalia in 1648, which ended the thirty-year-old religious conflict of central Eu-

---

14   Ibid
15   Sands P. and Klein P. (eds) Bowett's Law of International Institutions 5th edn (London: Sweet and Maxwell, 2001) p.1
16   Ibid
17   Potter S. An Introduction to the Study of International Organisations, 5th edn (New Zealand: Brooker's Auckland, 1948) p.130

rope and formally established the modern secular nation-State arrangement of European politics. [18]

The French Wars of Louis XIV were similarly brought to an end by an international agreement of interested powers, and a century later, the Napoleonic wars terminated with the congress of Vienna in 1815.[19] This latter conference can be taken as a significant turning point, for it marked the first systematic attempt to regulate international affairs by means of regular international conferences. The conference system lasted, in various guises, for practically a century and institutionalised not only the balance of power approach to politics, but also a semi-formal international order. Until the outbreak of the First World War, world affairs were to a large extent influenced by the periodic conferences that were held in Europe. The Paris Conference of 1856 and the Berlin Congress of 1871 dealt with the establishment and the repudiation of the regime for the Black Sea by Russia respectively; while the 1884-1885 Conferences were convened to attempt to regulate the "Scramble for Africa" which was leading commercial rivalry and political antagonism among the European powers.[20] The Hague Conference of 1899 and 1907 constituted an effort to secure, on multilateral basis, agreements on different aspects of the law relating to the conduct of warfare on land and on the sea, and on the duties of neutral States. [21]

The Congresses of Vienna, 1815 initiated the "concert system" which constituted a significant development. As sponsored by the Czar Alexander I, what was envisaged was an alliance of victorious powers pledged to conduct diplomacy accord-

18   Gross L. "The Peace of West Phalia, N. 1648-1948" AJIL (1948) p.20
19   Shaw M. N. op. cit. 888
20   Ibid
21   "Berlin West African Conference 1884-1885" EPIL p.389

ing to ethical standards, which would convene at congress held between 1818 and 1822 but the idea of regular congresses was abandoned and meetings took place as occasions required.[22] The attempt to secure regular meetings was however, a significant recognition that the pace of international relations demanded some institutions for regular multilateral negotiations. The "Concept of Europe" remained a quasi-institutionalized system even after the Holy Alliance had broken up, until the First World War destroyed the balance of power on which it rested.

As soluble as the conference system appeared to be, some commentators have argued that shortcomings overwhelmed the merits.[23] The argument cannot be faulted entirely. Some of the weaknesses garnered from the argument are: first, for each new problem which arose, a new conference had to be convened, generally on the initiative of one of the states concerned. The necessity of convening each conference anew complicated and delayed cooperation in dealing with the problem. Second, the conferences were not debating forums in the same way as the later assemblies of the League of Nations and the United Nations; delegations attended very much for the purposes of delivering statements of state policy and, though concessions were often made, the conferences had a rigidity which disappeared in the later "permanent" assemblies of the League and the United Nations. This position however, is debatable because the critics have failed to enumerate what constituted the rigidity which is not found in the latter institutions. It is therefore submitted that since the so-called rigidity has not been unearthed, the assertion is not wholly correct.

The third weakness or demerit associated with the conference system is that those conferences were held at the invitation

---

22   Shaw M.N. op. cit.
23   "Hague Peace Conferences 1899 and 1907", EPIL Vol. pp.671-677

of the sponsoring states; there was no principle of membership which conferred automatic right to representation or participation.[24] The deducible effect therefore is that, even though other states might have had problems demanding urgent international attention, since they were not invited by the sponsoring states, it was not possible for the participating States to look into such problems.

Another weakness considered by scholars as emanating from the conference system is that, the conferences adhered to the strict rule of equality, with the consequence that all States had an equal vote and all decisions required unanimity.[25] It is contended further that, it is now broadly accepted that there are a growing range of matters in which it is necessary to subjugate the will of the minority to that of the majority if progress is to be made, the dominance of unanimity rule represented a serious restriction on the powers of the ad-hoc conference.[26] This argument could best be described as a western ideology which does not represent the perception of the wider world.

The present position where the few "superlative powers" dictate for the majority like in the case of United Nations should not be encouraged. In every democratic environment, the equality of all should be promoted unlike the present situation in the United Nations wherein the few minority super-powers dictate for the whole universe. It is submitted that the Western ideology should not be promoted at the expense of the so-called developing nation-States.

Following the inadequacies of the conference system considered above, there was need for a paradigm shift as the representatives of the States at those conferences frequently did not

---

24   Sands P. and Klein op. cit. p.3
25   Sands P. and Klein P. Ibid p.3
26   Sands P. and Klein P. Ibid p.3

have the expertise to address technical issues in the developing areas of international trade, commerce, transportation and communication. This then called for permanent institutions which could tackle the emerging issues. The nineteenth century saw, therefore, an impressive development of associations or unions international in character between groups other than governments. This was followed by similar developments between governments themselves in the administrative field.[27] Since then, international institutions of varying degrees have continued to evolve with their personality distinct from the members.

Legal Personality of International Institutions

The essence of the role of international institutions in the world order centres on their possession of international legal personality. Once this is established, they become the subjects of international law and thus capable of enforcing rights and duties upon international plane as distinct from merely operating within the confines of separate municipal jurisdictions.[28] Not every co-operational arrangement between two or more States or between individuals per se or international organisations on the international plane that will necessarily establish legal personality. In the case of NAURA v. AUSTRALIA,[29] the International Court of Justice opined that the arrangement under which Australia, New Zealand and the United Kingdom became joint "Administering Authority" for Naura in the Trusteeship Agreement approved by the United Nations in 1947 did not establish a separate international legal personality distinct from that of the States.

---

27   Shaw M.N. op. cit. p.888
28   "International Law Association" EPIL vol.2 pp.1207-1208
29   Shaw M.N. op. cit. p.909

The concept of legal personality and its implications are not usually easy to identify. This seems to be particularly true in relation to international institutions, given that they are "secondary subjects" of international law, the creation of which flows from the will of other international persons, mostly States, and recently other international organisations.[30] The question of legal personality of the international institutions is for instance dependent upon the terms of the instrument establishing such institution. If the States wish the organisation to be endowed specifically with international legal personality, this will appear in the constituent instrument and will be determinative of the issue.[31]

Legal Personality Conferred by Constituent Instruments

International institutions generally perform legal activities in various legal orders, in each of these orders, the question of their legal personality arises. Therefore, in order to avoid carrying out the said activities in futility, the constituent instruments are said to have made provisions conferring legal personality on them. Some analysts have argued that the explicit conferment of international legal personality on "inter-governmental organisations" has for a long time remained the exception rather than the general rule.[32] This view is premised on the fact that the institutions would want to avoid being tagged "super-States". That being the case, international institutions prefers concluding bilateral instruments aiming at governing their status in the host countries and not in the main covenant. It was in this light that the League of Nations was recognised as possessing

---

30   Sand P. and Klein P. op. cit. p.470
31   Sand P. and Klein P. op. cit. p.470
32   See Article 6 of the European Coal and Steel Community Treaty, 1951 and Article 210 of the European Economic Community Treaty, 1951

international legal personality.[33] In the same vein, the United Nations Charter, apparently due to a wish to avoid any implication that the "United Nations was a super-State" only provides in Article 104 for the legal capacity of the organisation in the territory of its member-States.[34]

The vast majority of treaties establishing international institutions concluded after the Second World War likewise limit the recognition of legal personality to the domestic sphere of member States. The explicit attribution of legal personality to the international institutions has, however, become much more frequent since then included in the constituent instruments. [35]Such constituent instruments include the 1976 Agreement establishing International Fund for Agricultural Development which confers legal personality on the organisation under Article 10 Section 1. The treaty establishing Economic Community of West African States (ECOWAS), 1993 has equally attributed legal personality to the institution under Article 88. It has been contended that this evolution reflects the changes in the international society itself, which is increasingly open to the co-existence of various categories of subject of international law.[36]

In some cases, the legal personality of international institutions is inferred from the powers or purposes of the organisation and its practice. This was the position of the International Court of Justice in its Advisory opinion in **Reparation for Injuries Suffered in the Services of the United Nations Case,**[37] where it held that the United Nations had international legal

33 Montaldo R. "International Legal Personality and Implied Powers of International Organisations" 44 BYBIL (1970), pp.111-155

34 Official Journal of the League of Nations Vol.7, 1926

35 Report to the President on the Results of the San Francisco Conference, Department of State Publication 2349, (1945) series 71, 157

36 See Article 6 of the Treaty establishing European Coal and Steel Community, 1951

37 Sands P. and Klein P. op. cit. p.471

personality because this was indispensable in order to achieve the purposes and specified in the charter. The court stated as follows:

> *The organisation was intended to exercise and enjoy, and is in fact enjoying and exercising, functions and rights which can only be explained on the basis of the possession of a large measure of international personality and capacity to operate upon an international plane. It is at present the supreme type of international organisation and could not carry out the intentions of its founders if it was devoid of international personality. It must be acknowledged that its members, by entrusting certain functions to it, with attendant duties and responsibilities, have clothed it with the competence required to enable those functions to be effectively discharged.*[38]

The decision of the court in the above case is essentially inductive. The court's decision was based on the observation of the conferment of specific legal capacities on the organisation as such and of particular functions which could not practically be out if the organisation did not possess judicial personality in the international sphere. As sound as the position of the court may appear to be, it seems the court has rather made the organisation a "super-State" by referring to it as "the supreme type of international organisation" contrary to the spirit behind the provisions of Article 104 of the organisation's charter.

The conferment of legal personality on the international institutions brings into being what would have been a lifeless body, thereby having all the rights, duties and responsibilities.

---

38   ICJ Reports, 1949, p.174

From the decision of the court in the **Reparation**[39] it is essential to note that, the judges took great care to link the attribution of such personality to the wiles of the member-States, in case of inter-governmental organisation or that of the individual members, in case of private international institutions, which is necessarily implied in this case. The judicial recognition or attribution of legal personality to United Nations in the above case has been widely adapted to virtually all international organisations even when such provision is not found in the constituent or other instruments.[40]

Undebatably, by creating the "potential capacity", the attribution of legal personality to an international institution establishes it as an entity legally distinct from its members. This was emphasised by the International Court of Justice in its Advisory opinion in 1949, when it noted that "(P)ractice – in particular the conclusion of conventions in which the organisation is a party – has confirmed this character of the organisation, which occupies a position in certain respects in detachment of its members..."[41]

Some scholars have argued that while the international legal personality of an international institution imposes itself on its members, the same cannot be said for non-members. It is contended further that they (the third States) are free to acknowledge such international legal personality either expressly or implicitly, for instance, by concluding a treaty with the organisation, or to disregard it and to affirm their preference for the establishment of legal relation with the members exclusive-

39 Supra at 179
40 Supra
41 Schermers J. and Blokker T. International Institution Law 3rd edn (London: Nijhoff Press, 1995) p.1568

ly.[42] With respect to the respected authors, this argument does not hold water in all situations. There are situations where international institutions, especially United Nations, compel non-members to observe the organisation's acts or even observe her charter which they are not signatories thereto. Article 2(6) of the United Nations charter provides that "the organisation shall ensure that States which are not members of the United Nations act in accordance with these principles so far as may be necessary for the maintenance of international peace and security." It has been rightly contended that "this provision creates binding obligation rather than being merely a statement of attitude with regard to non-members of the United Nations."[43] This again conforms to the earlier submission that United Nations could best be regarded as a "super-State" contrary to the provisions of Article 104 of the charter. It is submitted that non-recognition of legal personality of international institution by non-members or third parties does not apply to United Nations, therefore to make a sweeping assertion that third states will not recognise the legal personality of an international institution is not wholly correct.

Legal Personality Conferred by Domestic Laws

The attribution of legal personality to international organisations is not only on the international sphere or plane, it is also recognised at the domestic or national level. This recognition is, albeit, created by the constituent instruments establishing such international organisations.[44] These instruments have often been supplemented by more specific instruments, such as multilateral conventions or protocols specifying the le-

---

42   See Reparation Case (Supra)
43   Sands P. and Klein P. op. cit. p.476
44   Shaw M.N. op. cit. p.652

gal status and detailing the privileges and immunities of one or more organisations, or bilateral treaties concluded between one organisation and its host State to further define the organisation's legal status in the country, that is, headquarters agreement.[45] It is posited that the instruments providing for an organisation's personality in the domestic sphere usually specify that the organisation has the capacity to conclude contracts, acquire and dispose of movable and immovable property, and to institute legal proceedings, these being viewed as essential to the proper functioning of any international organisation.[46] The legal personality of international institutions in domestic legal orders encompasses the power to perform any legal act or function that would prove to be necessary for the organisation to fulfil its mission. It is contended further that, it may safely be said that even in the absence of any explicit instrument or provision of that kind, any international organisation must be deemed to enjoy an independent legal personality in domestic orders, since this will almost always prove necessary to enable it discharge its functions on daily basis.

The attribution of legal personality to international organisations is to enable them create impacts on the domestic legal orders. This attribution and recognition of the legal capacity of the international institutions is not strange to member-States because as a rule of international law, they are bound by the treaties they are parties thereto. In fact, in monist States such as Netherlands, treaties are given precedence over national legislations.[47] Even in dualist States such as Nigeria, it only takes a long process by domesticating such treaties by legislative en-

---

45   See Article 12(1) of the World Property International Organisation; Article 21(1) of the United Nations Industrial Development Organisation, etc.
46   See Sands P. and Klein P. op. cit. p.477
47   Ibid.

actments[48] but once they are enacted into law, such States are bound thereby. In either of the above cases, member States are bound to attribute legal personality to international institutions wherein they have membership.

On the other hand, the situation is slightly different in non-member States, since these are not under obligation per se to give effect to a legal personality deriving from an international instrument which they are not parties thereto.[49] However, in the vast majority of cases, the legal personality of international institution is recognised in national courts of non-member States by application of their conflict-of-laws rules, or by the principle of "comity." Courts therefore, tend to apply to "foreign" international institutions the same principle as the one they would use when called upon to pronounce the legal personality of foreign corporations.[50] Since, unlike foreign corporations, international institutions are not "incorporated" under the laws of a particular state, it is to the international norms proclaiming the institutions legal personality that national courts ought logically to turn to give effect to this personality in a non-member's domestic legal order. The recognition of legal personality as deriving directly from international law is said to have been however, treated with circumspection in some domestic legal orders. For instance, in ARAB MONETARY FUND v. HASHIM (NO.3)[51] the House of Lords took a very different path to recognise the legal personality of an international institution to which United Kingdom was not a party in basing this recognition on comity and on the fact that the organisation concerned had been given legal

---

48   See the case of BOSCH V. DE GEUS case 13/61, (1962) C.M.L.R.I
49   See Section 12 of the Constitution of the Federal Republic of Nigeria, 1999 ; GANI
     FAWEHIMNI v. ABACHA (2006) 6 NWLR (Pt.660) p.228
50   Sands P. and Klein P. op. cit. p.478
51   Ibid

personality and capacity by the law of the State wherein it has seat or permanent location.

From the preceding discussion, it is axiomatic that, unlike human beings, international institutions are conceived lifeless until they are accorded "the life" which confers legal personality on them. Once the constituent instrument confers the legal capacity on them, they become distinct from their members, and they can perform their functions in their names in accordance with their mandate. This personality comes with privileges and immunities to enable them perform their functions without being hindered.

Privileges and Immunities of International Institutions

For effective performance, states and their representatives benefit from a variety of privileges and immunities. In the same vein, international institutions are also granted privileges and immunities for their assets, property and representatives. Scholars have contended that the two situations (the immunities of both States and international institutions) are not, of course, analogous in practice, since the basis of immunities may be seen in terms of the sovereign equality of states and reciprocity, while it is not realistic with regard to international institutions, both because they are not in a position of "sovereign equality and because they are unable to grant immunity as reciprocal gesture. It is also the case that the immunities of states have been restricted in the light of the distinction between *"transactions Jure Imperii and Jure Gestionis,"*[52] while any such distinction in the case of international institutions would be inappropriate.[53] Since the purpose of this research is not to examine the immunities of States, it is inappropriate to delve

---

52   February 21 (1991) 85 ILR 8-9
53   Shaw M.N. op. cit. pp.923-924; See BRANNO v. MINISTRY OF WAR 22 ILR P.756

into arguments in that regard, therefore, the discussion herein will be centred on the immunities of international institutions.

The true basis for the immunities accorded to the international institutions is that they are necessitated by the effective exercise of their functions. The question that is to be raised is how can the immunities of the international institutions be measured in the light of such functional necessity? To resolve this issue, the immunities will be measured in the circumstances of the functions each of them will perform, and in accordance with the provisions of their constituent instruments and other supplemental instruments as well as diplomatic relations. For instance, Article 105(1) of the United Nations charter provides that "the organisation shall enjoy in the territory of each of its members such privileges and immunities as are necessary for the fulfilment of its purpose." This and other provisions as contained in the above article are supplemented by General Convention on the Privileges and Immunities of the United Nations 1946, and the Convention on Privileges and Immunities of Specialised Agencies, 1947. These two conventions formed a model for latter agreements made by other international institutions.[54]

It has been argued that these agreements are of a multilateral character, it has often been found necessarily a bilateral agreement with the host States in whose territory the headquarters or other offices of the institutions are maintained.[55] The Headquarters Agreement between United Nations and the United States of America, and United Nations and Switzerland are good examples of such agreements. Special agreements, which provide for privileges and immunities for the institutions and their agents, are also frequently concluded by international institutions with states on the territory of which they undertake

---

54   Higgins R. Problems and Process (Oxford: Oxford Press, 1994) p.93
55   See Article viii(4) of the World Trade Organisation Convention.

particular activities, such as the provision of technical assistance or the establishment of peacekeeping operations.[56] Clearly, these agreements, whether multilateral or bilateral, impose legal obligation on States under international law. Since privileges and immunities will by their very nature need to produce their effects within the domestic legal order of member States, it is necessary for these to ensure that those legal rights and obligations are domestically enforceable. States often implement these obligations by passing municipal or local legislation. The International Organisations Immunities Act of December, 1949 in the United States International Organisation (Privileges and immunities) Act of July, 1950 in the United Kingdom are typical examples of such legislations.

One pertinent question that readily comes to mind here is whether in the absence of a treaty agreement or obligation, a State is under any duty to concede privileges and immunities to an international institution? Some commentators have posited that it is difficult to argue that all international institutions are to enjoy privileges and immunities by virtue of a rule of customary international law.[57] It is well settled that the privileges and immunities of United Nations is generally accepted by a principle of international customary law.[58] A more liberal view has been taken by some governments and national courts considering that international institutions were entitled to jurisdictional immunity under customary international law.[59]

The main privileges and immunities accorded to international organisations are immunities from jurisdiction, execu-

---

56 Sands P. and Klein P. op. cit. p.488
57 See the Agreement between United Nations and Kuwait concerning the legal status, privileges and immunities of the UN Iraq-Kuwait Mission, April 15-May 20 1992 UNJY (1992) p.71
58 Sands P. and Klein P. op. cit. p.489
59 See the view taken by the UN Office of Legal Affairs, UNJY (1976) p.179

tion, inviolabilities of premises and archive, currency and fiscal privileges and freedom from communications. This position is clearly provided for under Article IV, section 11 of the United Nations General Convention, 1946; it is provided that the representatives of states shall have:

(a)　*immunity from personal arrest or detention and from seizure of their personal baggage, and in respect of words spoken or written and all acts done by them in their capacities as representatives, immunity from legal process of every kind;*

(b)　*inviolability for all parts and documents;*

(c)　*the right to use codes and to receive papers or correspondence by courier or in sealed bags;*

(d)　*exemption in respect of themselves and their spouses from immigration restrictions, alien registration or national service obligations in the states they are visiting or through which they are passing in the exercise of their functions;*

(e)　*the same facilities in respect of currency or exchange restrictions as are accorded to representatives of foreign governments on temporary official mission;*

(f)　*the same immunities and facilities in respect of their personal baggage as are accorded to diplomatic envoys; and also*

(g)　*such other privileges, immunities and facilities not inconsistent with the foregoing as diplomatic envoys enjoy, except that they shall have no right to claim exemption from custom duties on goods imported (otherwise than as*

*part of their personal baggage) or from excise
duties or sales taxes.*

The rationale for according privileges and immunities to international institutions is provided for under Article IV section 14 of the convention wherein privileges and immunities are accorded as follows:

> *...in order to safeguard the independent exercise
> of their functions in connection with the United Nations. Consequently a member not only has the right
> but is under a duty to waive the immunity of its representative in any case where in the opinion of the
> member the immunity would impede the course of
> justice, and it can be waived without prejudice to
> the purpose for which the immunity is accorded.*

The International Court of Justice has lent its voice by way of advisory opinion concerning the applicability of the provisions in the General Convention to Special Rapporteurs appointed by the sub-commission on the prevention of Discrimination and Protection of Minorities.[60] Article VI, section 22 of the Convention provides that experts performing missions for the United Nations are to be accorded such privileges and immunities as are necessary for the independent exercise of their functions during the period of their missions. The International Court noted further that such privileges and immunities could indeed be invoked against the State nationality or residence (subject to principle of reservation) and that Rapporteurs for the sub-commission were to be regarded as experts on mission within the meaning of section 22 of the convention. The essence

---

60   See IRAN – USCTR v. AS (1985) 94 ILR 327

of privileges and immunities accorded in international institutions is graphically captured as follows:

> *The proper measure of international immunities is what is necessary for the impartial, efficient and economic discharge of the functions of the organisation concerned, and in particular what contributes to the effective independence of the organisation from the individual control of its separate members exercised by means of their national law and executive authority as distinguished from their collective control exercised in a regular manner through the appropriate international organs.* [61]

This view indubitably remains accurate, and points to the need for a balance between requirements of efficient and independent functioning of the international institutions, on one hand, and the necessity of justice being done, on the other hand. The fact that the immunities accorded to international institutions is procedural only, which by no means prevent international institutions and their agents from complying with law applicable to their activities, should never be overlooked. It is based on the premise that exceptions are attached to the immunities and privileges of international institutions. These exceptions come in the form of contractual obligations wherein parties, including international institutions, are bound by the terms therein. Article 288 of the European Community Treaty provides that *"the contractual liability of the community shall be governed by the law applicable to the contract in question."* This shows that international institutions may be held liable for any

---

[61] The Applicability of Article vi, section 22 of the convention on privilege and immunities of the United Nations, ICI Reports (1989) p.77

violation or breach of terms of contracts they entered into, irrespective of privileges and immunities.

Besides, international institutions may be held liable for tortuous acts done by their agents in carrying out their official duties. Article 22 Annex iii of the United Nations Convention on the Law of the Seas (UNCLOS III, 1982) states that the International Sea-Bed Authority will have the "responsibility or liability for any damage arising out of wrongful acts in the exercise of its powers and functions..." The organisations may also waive their privileges and immunities but such waiver must be provided for in the constituent instruments establishing them.[62] As the International Court of Justice rightly pointed out in its Advisory Opinion in 1999, the question of immunity from legal process is distinct from the issue of compensation for any damages incurred as a result of acts performed by the United Nations or by its agents acting in their official capacity. This, therefore shows that despite the privileges and immunities accorded international institutions, they may be held liable where they fail to comply with the requirements of law governing their relations with other people or states. It is patently clear that such immunities are not absolute in the interest of peaceful co-existence.

Liability and Personality of International Institutions
The legal personality, privileges and immunities conferred on the international institutions to enable them perform effectively and efficiently, are accompanied by responsibilities or liabilities. It has been submitted that from the theoretical point of view, the fact that international institutions may be held accountable for the consequences of their illegal or wrongful acts is widely accepted. The liability is thus generally presented as

62   Jenks O. International Immunities (London: Steven and Sons Press, 1961) pp.41-42

the logical collory of the powers and rights conferred upon international organizations.[63] This position was graphically captured by the United Nations Secretary-General when he put it that *"the international responsibility of the United Nations for the activities of the United Nations forces is an attribution of its international legal personality and its capacity to bear international rights and obligations."* [64] In FRANCE v. COMMISSION, [65]the European Court of Justice held that the non-performance of an international agreement by the Commission could make the community liable at the international level.

From the above position therefore, it is indeed clear that the responsibility of an international institution may flow from a breach of the rules governing the activities of the international institutions and pertaining to their own legal order, domestic legal orders and indeed the international law at large. As considered in the proceeding discussion, and will be considered subsequently, the rules governing the liability regime within each of these legal systems are applicable to international institutions, as any other subjects of the system concerned.

Liability Arising from International Law

As noted earlier in the prelude under this subheading, responsibility or liability is a necessary consequence of international personality and the resulting possession of international rights and duties. Such rights and duties may flow from treaties, headquarters agreements or from principles of international customary law.[66] In the case of **Reparation for Injuries**

---

63   See Section 22 of Article iv of the United Nations General Convention, 1946
64   Sand P. and Klein P. op. cit. p.513
65   See the Report on the "Administrative and the Budgetary Aspects of the Financing of the United Nations Peace Keeping Operations" Doc. A/57/389, September 20, 1996, paragraph 6.
66   Case C-327/91 (1994) 1 – 3674 p.25

suffered in the Services of the United Nations,[67] the International Court of Justice opined that the obligations entered into by member-States to enable the agents of the United Nations to perform their obligations were obligations owed to the organisation, therefore the organisation had the capacity to claim adequate reparation, and that in assessing this reparation it is authorised to pay the damages suffered by the victim or persons entitled through him. Just as a state can be held responsible for injury to an organisation or its agents, so can an international institution be held liable for an injury to a state or its citizens where the injury arises out of a breach by an international institution of an international obligation deriving from a treaty provision or principle of customary international law. As the United Nations Secretary-General succinctly puts it:

> The international responsibility of the United Nations is a reflection of the principle of state responsibility widely accepted to be applicable to international organisation – that damage caused in breach of an international obligation and which is attributed to the state (or of the organisation) entails the international responsibility and its liability in compensation. [68]

From the above statement, it is indubitably axiomatic that the elements of state responsibility, that is to say, breach of an international obligation and attribution of wrongful act to the State apply equally to the determination of an international institution's responsibility. Examples of the international liability of international institutions abound especially regarding the internationally wrongful acts committed in the context of peace-keeping operations. For instance, the United Nations Opera-

---

67   See the World Health Organization Regional Office case, ICI Reports (1980) p.73
68   (Supra)

41

tion in the Congo (UNOC) during which extensive damage was caused to civilians of various nationalities by the United Nations forces in the 1960s, undoubtedly constituted a most significant precedent. The United Nations accepted responsibility for those acts, and compensated the victims and some agreements were concluded with the States concerned.[69] Again, the international responsibility of an international institution was evoked in relation to the bombing of Yugoslavia in 1999.[70] In view of the above therefore, it is undoubtedly clear that the international institutions are held liable for the wrongful acts done in breach of any international obligation arising either from the treaties to which they are signatories or from customary international law.

Liability Arising from the Internal Laws of the International Institutions

Apart from the international law obligations which bind international institutions, the breach of which renders them liable, their internal laws equally bind them, and any breach of such laws will result in the responsibility of such an organisation. It has been argued that illegal acts of international institutions will devoid any legal effect, therefore when they produce adverse consequences, they may make the organisation liable to compensate for the damages caused. This argument is apposite because when an international organisation acts outside its mandate, any consequential effect should be borne by it.

The internal laws of a few international institutions extend this liability to all damages caused by organs or agents in the cause of their functions, thus covering the consequences of their legislative or executive activities. The most developed of

---

69   See the Report in footnote 51
70   See the Agreements relating to settlement of claims filed against United Nations in the Congo concluded with Belgium, February 20, 1965, 535 UNTS 197

systems is found in the European Community.[71] Article 288(2) of the Rome Treaty provides that "in the case of non-contractual liability, the community shall, in accordance with the general principles common to the laws of the member States, make good any damage caused by its institutions or by its servants in the performance of their duties." The creation of this regime of non-contractual liability finds its justification in the desire to ensure that the transfer of powers by member States to the community would not entail the withdrawal of the guarantees conferred upon private persons under national laws to be compensated for damages caused by national authorities in the exercise of their functions. This regime applies to the consequences of administrative or executive as well as legislative activities of institutions, though under very restrictive conditions.

It is common to find internal rules of the international institutions providing for the liability of such international organisations towards their staff, for service incurred damages.[72] These include damages resulting from accidents, natural catastrophes, as operations among others. Apart from the above situations, the liability of international institutions could find root in the domestic laws of member States wherein they operate.

Liability Arising from Domestic Laws

Since international institutions are to comply with legislations in force in the countries on the territory of which they carry out their activities, it is logical that breaches of domestic rules should entail the liability of the institutions in accordance with relevant domestic laws. As stated earlier, it is the institutions' capability to hold rights and obligations in those legal

---

71   See the Report submitted to the United Nations' authorities by the Independent Commission of Inquiry on December 16, 1999 Doc.S/1999/1257
72   Sands P. and Klein P. op. cit. p.514

orders which engender their responsibility for the consequences of unlawful acts. In reality, liability may arise either under contracts concluded by international institutions, and to which a national law is applicable, or in circumstances where tortuous acts are attributable to an organisation irrespective of any contractual link. For instance, most contracts of Universal Postal Union and some of those of the World Health Organisation are governed by Swiss laws, whereas those of the International Civil Aviation Organisation are governed by laws of the Province of Quebec. For the Organisation of American States, the law of the District of Columbia governs contracts carried out at the seat of the organisation, whereas in the case of contracts performed in the territory of other members, it is that local law that applies.[73]

The fact that the contractual liability of international institutions is governed by law applicable to the contract itself, usually national law, is not indisputable. Organisations may, in such cases, find themselves liable as a result of non-performance of the contractual clauses, as would any other party to such contract.[74] The position was upheld in the WESTLAND case.[75] In that case, disagreements between the member States of the Arab Organisation for Industrialisation (AOI) led to the suspension of the organisation's activities, which in turn entailed the non-fulfilment of a large-scale joint-venture contract, governed by the Swiss law, concluded with the British company, Westland Helicopters. Westland initiated proceedings against the organisation and its members before the Court of Arbitration of the International Chamber of Commerce, and after sev-

---

73 Ibid.
74 See the position of the Community Court in Vloeberghs v. High Authority, VII Rep. 449. The extension of this regime to legislative activities was first affirmed in Schollensted case (case5/71, December 2, 1971) p.70
75 See Article II(a) of Appendix D of the UN Staff Rules (Doc. St. SGB Staff Rules Appendix D Rev. I, 1966)

eral procedures before Swiss tribunals, was ultimately awarded compensation in 1993.

The liability of international institutions under national law for damages resulting from their activities on the territory of a State is beyond dispute, and applies to contractual as well as non-contractual damages, that is, tortuous liability.[76] In order to protect themselves against the consequences of non-contractual liability, international institutions generally conclude insurance contracts with private companies.[77] In case of short-term activities such as conferences, they enter into agreement with the host States providing for the transfer of liability, or more specifically, of the consequences of such liability to that State.[78] While implementation of the liability of international institutions before national courts may be limited by the jurisdictional immunity usually granted to internationally inflicted results directly, unless other mechanisms have been put in such as insurance transfer of liability to the host State inter alia.

From the above discourse, it is patently incontrovertible that despite the immunities and privileges accorded international institutions, they would be held liable whenever they go outside their mandate. Even when they act within the purview of their mandate, they may be held responsible for the injury occasioned to their staff in the course of their official duties.

Dissolution of International Institutions

Since nothing is permanent except change, international institutions being "living" entities with attributes of privileges, immunities as well as liabilities, may undergo significant

---

76   Sands P and Klein P op. cit. p.462
77   Lysen S. The Non-Contractual and Contractual Liability of European Communities
      (Stockholm: Almgvist and Wiksell Publishers, 1976) p.155
78   Court of Arbitration of International Chamber of Commerce, June 23, 1993 (unreported)

changes or even dissolve completely. An international institution's existence may come to an end when its members decide that it has completed its purpose, or that the circumstances do not make it possible for it to continue functioning as in the case of the then Organisation of African Unity. Instances where the institutions terminated completely without succession include the East African Community in 1977,[79] even though the organisation was revived in 1986 in the form of Commission for East African Cooperation, it was dissolved in 1991 due to political changes in the Pact's member States and to the overall evolution of Europe's geopolitical landscape, and the Intergovernmental Bureau for Informatics that was also dissolved in the same year, 1991.[80] In another situation however, the functions of an institution, the existence of which is brought to an end, are transferred to another institution which could be described as its "successor". The dissolution of the predecessor institution is in such cases followed or accompanied by a succession process described as the "transfer of functions and their ancillary rights and obligations from one organisation to the other.[81] Examples of such succession include the replacement of the International Commission for Air by International Civil Aviation Organisation in 1994 and the metamorphosis of the Organisation of African Unity into African Union (the focal point herein) in 2002.

Whether or not the constituent instrument provides for dissolution of an international institution, circumstances may arise which will inevitably compel it to be dissolved. It has been argued that it is somewhat unlikely in the case of organisa-

---

79   It should be noted that tortuous liability of international institutions as considered earlier, is governed by national laws only when and to the extent that the institutions have not adopted specific rules to that effect in their internal legal order

80   This sometime specifically provide for under Headquarters Agreements

81   See Article XIII of the Agreement of January 29, 1992 between UN and Columbia on the arrangement for 8th session of UNCTAD, UNJY (1992) p.20

tions such as United Nations, mostly specialised agencies, the European Community and other important regional organisations to anticipate dissolution since permanence is the aim.[82] It is submitted with respect that such argument does not hold water entirely. This is because at the global level, the League of Nations was formed with the aim of being permanent but unavoidably, it dissolved following the outbreak of the Second World War. Again, the Organisation of African Unity was formed with the aim of being perpetually in existence, however, with the dawn of the new millennium, the member States realised that it could not meet the yearnings and aspirations of the continent. This therefore, led to the formation of African Union, which is believed to be the "emancipator" of the continent. Flowing from the above submissions, it is unarguably incontrovertible that any international institution could be dissolved depending on the facts of each case.

Whether one international institution has been dissolved completely or replaced by a new legal entity, depends upon the intention of the members as reflected in the instrument effecting the constitutional change. For instance, the changes to the Constitution of the Universal Postal Union as between 1874, 1878 and 1957 were regarded simply as amendments. However, the International Tele-Commissions Union Convention of 1932, replacing the 1865 Convention created a new legal entity which fused the personality of the old International Tele-Communications Union with the new Radio-Telegraphic Union.[83] In practice, the fact remains that even in the absence of specific provision(s) governing dissolution in the constituent instrument of an institution, it is "good evidence that there is a general

---

82   Sands P. and Klein P. op. cit. p.258. The organisation functioned until 1977 when I ceased its activities due to political differences between the member states.
83   Ibid p.530

principle of the international institutions law (though not codi-
fied) that an organization may be dissolved by the decision of its
highest representative body." [84]

The above discussion has clearly shown that since international institutions are "living things", whether there are provisions in their various constituent instruments regarding dissolution or not, depending on the circumstances of each case,
may be dissolved at a particular point in time. It was through
this process of dissolution that African Union, the essence of
this book, emerged by succeeding its predecessor, Organisation
of African Unity, and inherited all its institutions or structures,
rights, privileges, immunities and liabilities.

---

84 Amerasignghe J. Principles of the International Law of International Organisations
(Cambridge: C.U.P 1996) 471

CHAPTER THREE

International Institutions in Africa

Introduction

The African Union is a successor to the Organisation of African Unity (OAU), the intergovernmental organisation for African States in existence since 1963, created with the aim of strengthening integration among member States, and the voice of African Continent in global affairs. With the end of the Cold War, the final liberation of Africa and the reshaping of international political scene, African Heads of State recognised that the Organisation of African Unity (hereinafter called OAU) framework was not adequate to meet the needs for greater intercontinental policy coordination and stronger economic growth, and that a greater commitment to democratic government at national level was necessary to strengthen Africa's own voice on the international stage. Then the stage was set for the introduction of a new born baby, African Union, "the Messiah of the continent". The envisaged new body was to be structured after the European Union's institutional framework.

The constitutive Act of the African Union, its founding document, was adopted by the Heads of State in Lome, Togo, and entered into force in 2001. The Union, however, took off officially in July, 2002 with its inaugural meeting held in Durban, South Africa.[85] The Union has 53 member States, only Morocco that is not a member among the States on the continent, be-

---

85   Chitiga R. "Strengthening Popular Participation in the African Union. A guide to AU Structures and Processes", Publication of an Open Society Institutive Network, 2009

49

cause it withdrew from the then OAU in 1984 to protest the admission of Sahrawi Arab Democratic Republic (Western Sahara) as a member of the organisation.

African Union has embedded African Economic Community, which was established by a treaty adopted in Abuja, Nigeria, in 1991 and became part of its predecessor, as part of its system. The constitutive Act of the Union and the Treaty of African Economic Community, are said to be complementary, and jointly provide the legal basis for continental integration.[86] Most of the key organs of the Union are established under its constitutive Act but some are set under Protocols to the constitutive Act or the Abuja Treaty establishing the African Economic Community, free-standing treaties or other legal documentation.[87] Both the constitutive Act and the Abuja Treaty are said to be capable of putting African Continent on the pedestal of globalisation, and indeed the needed development.

The Historical Development of the African Union

The African Union being a successor institution historically inherited its base from the predecessor, Organisation of African Unity. For a better understanding, it is appropriate to look at the historical background of the Union in order to examine its performance in line with the spirit behind its formation. As noted earlier, the Organisation of African Unity was established on 25th May, 1963 in Addis Ababa, on signature of OAU Charter by representatives of 32 governments.[88] A further 21 States joined gradually over the years, with South Africa becoming the 53rd member in 1994. Analysts posited that as far back

---

86 Ibid p.4

87 See for instance Article 5 of the African Union Constitutive Act

88 Transition from the OAU to African Union, retrieved from http://www.au2002.gov.za/docs/background/oau-to-au html Retrieved on 7th July, 2010

as 1970 it became evident and accepted, where committee on the Review of the OAU charter was established that, a need existed to amend the organisation's charter, in order to streamline the organisation to gear it more accurately for the challenges of a changing world.[89] Despite numerous meetings, the Charter Review Committee did not manage to formulate substantive amendments.

However, the result of the Committee's work was threefold: the charter was "amended" by being augmented through ad-hoc decisions of the summit such as the Cairo Declaration establishing the mechanism for conflict prevention, management and resolution; a growing realisation that the need for greater efficiency and effectiveness of the organisation required urgent action; and to integrate the political activities of the Organisation of African Unity with economic and development issues as articulated in the Abuja Treaty.[90] Since the entry into force of the Abuja Treaty establishing the African Economic Community, the organisation had been operating on the two legal instruments, that is to say, the OAU charter and the Abuja Treaty. The Abuja Treaty came into force after the requisite number of ratification in May, 1994. It provided for African Economic Community to be set up through a gradual process which could be achieved by coordination, harmonisation and progressive integration of the activities of existing and future regional economic organisations.

As the 20th Century gradually came to an end, there were agitations that Africa needed a stronger institution to meet the emerging challenges facing the continent. It was by acclamation that the Assembly of Heads of State and Government in July 1999 in Algiers accepted an invitation from Colonel Mua-

---

89   Ibid
90   Ibid

mmar Gadhafi to the 4th Extraordinary Summit in September, 1999, in Sirte, Libya. The purpose for the Extraordinary Summit was to amend the OAU charter to increase the efficiency and effectiveness of the organisation. The theme of the summit was "Strengthening OAU Capacity to enable it Meet the Challenges of the New Millennium".[91] This summit concluded on the 9th September, 1999, with Sirte Declaration aimed at:

> *Effectively addressing the new social, political and economic realities in Africa and the world;*
>
> *Fulfilling the people's aspirations for greater unity in conforming to the objectives of the OAU charter and the Treaty establishing the African Economic Community;*
>
> *Eliminating the scourge of conflict;*
>
> *Meeting global challenges; and harnessing the human and natural resources of the continent to improve living condition.*[92]

To achieve the above aims, the summit *inter alia* decided to establish an African Union in conformity with the ultimate objectives of the charter of the continental organisation and the provisions of the treaty establishing the African Economic Community. It was also agreed to accelerate the process for the implementation of the treaty establishing African Economic Community in particular by shortening the implementation period of Abuja Treaty; ensuring the speedy establishment of all the institutions provided for Abuja Treaty such as the African Central Bank, the African Monetary Union, the African Court of Justice

---

91   Ibid
92   Reports on International Organisations, A Publication of American Society of International Law P.1 retrieved from file; //overcome-d6a71a/shared/the%20 African%20(AU). htm on 2/10/2010

and in particular, the Pan-African Parliament. Strengthening and consolidating the Regional Economic Communities as the pillars for achieving the objectives of African Economic Community and realising the envisaged Union's objectives and to convene an African Ministerial Conference on Security, Stability, Development and Cooperation in the continent, as soon as possible.[93] It was in the wake of the foregoing that the constitutive Act of African Union was adopted by the African Heads of State in Lome, Togo in July, 2000. The new Union came with the mandate to fulfil the objectives and the aims contained in its Act and other eventualities in the continent.

Objectives and Principles of the African Union

Change in every situation comes with new principles, objectives and ideologies which the proponents of such a change consider to be better than the old order. Whatever name given to it, transformation, transfiguration or metamorphosis, the old order is changed at least in form, even though the substance may be same. This applies to African Union and its predecessor, OAU. Whereas the purpose set out in the OAU charter focussed on the defence of the sovereignty, territorial integrity and independence of African States as well as the eradication of all forms of colonialism from Africa, the African Union has broader set of objectives and principles which are considered herein seriatim.

In general, the African Union objectives are different and to some extent more comprehensive than those of the Organisation of African Unity. Some scholars have posited that at the time African Union was formed, the organisation "had served its mission and was due for replacement by a structure geared towards addressing the current needs of the continent."[94] This po-

---

93   Ibid
94   See Transition from the OAU to the African Union op. cit. p.2

sition stems from the fact that since the organisation's objective of emancipating the continent from the shackles of colonialism was achieved, it could not serve any other purpose even though the other objectives such as promotion of unity and solidarity of African States, defence of the member States' sovereignty, territorial integrity and independence among others were still achievable. It is submitted that the change in nomenclature is not a solution to the problems militating against the continent. This is because most of the problems or difficulties encountered by the organisation still remain unresolved. In reality, the metamorphosis is a mere camouflage in that all the structures of the organisation were inherited by the Union with little or no modification.

As contained in the constitutive Act of the African Union, the objectives of the Union shall be to:

a.   *Achieve greater unity and solidarity between African countries and the peoples of Africa;*

b.   *Defend the sovereignty, territorial integrity and independence of its member States;*

c.   *Accelerate the political and socio-economic integration of the continent;*

d.   *Promote and defend African common positions on issues of interest to the continent and its peoples;*

e.   *Encourage international cooperation; taking due account of the charter of the United Nations and the Universal Declaration of Human Rights;*

f.   *Promote peace, security and stability on the continent;*

g. Promote democratic principles and institutions, popular participation and good governance;

h. Promote and protect human and peoples' rights in accordance with the African Charter on Human and Peoples Rights and other relevant human rights instruments;

i. Establish the necessary conditions which enable the continent to play its rightful role in the global economy and in international negotiations;

j. Promote sustainable development at the economic, social and cultural levels as well as the integration of African economies;

k. Promote cooperation in all fields of human activity to raise the living standard of African peoples;

l. Coordinate and harmonise policies between existing and future Regional Economic Communities for the gradual attainment of the objectives of the Union;

m. Advance the development of the continent by promoting research in all fields, in particular in science and technology;

n. Work with relevant international partners in the eradication of preventable diseases and the promotion of good health on the continent.[95]

---

95   See Article 3 of the Constitutive Act of the African Union

For easy and better achievement of the Union's objectives, the constitutive Act of the Union has laid down the principle upon which they could be attained. Article 4 of the Act has provided that the Union shall function in accordance with the following principles:

a.   *Sovereign equality and interdependence among member states of the union;*

b.   *Respect of borders existing on achievement of independence;*

c.   *Participation of the African peoples in the activities of the Union;*

d.   *Establishment of a common defence policy for African continent;*

e.   *Peaceful resolution of conflict among member States of the Union through such appropriate means as may be decided upon by the Assembly;*

f.   *Prohibition of the use of force or threat to use force among member States of the Union;*

g.   *Non-interference by any member State in the internal affairs of another;*

h.   *The right of the Union to intervene in a member State pursuant to a decision of the Assembly in respect of grave circumstances, namely war crimes, genocide and crime against humanity;*

i.   *Peaceful co-existence of member States and their right to live in peace and security;*

j.   *The right of member State to request intervention from the Union in order to restore peace and security;*

k.   *Promotion of self-reliance within the framework of the Union;*

l.   *Promotion of gender equality;*

m.   *Respect for democratic principles, human rights, the rule of law and good governance;*

n.   *Promotion of social justice to ensure balanced economic development;*

o.   *Respect for the sanctity of human life, condemnation and rejection of impunity and political assassination, acts of terrorism and subversive activities; and*

p.   *Condemnation and rejection of unconstitutional changes of government.*

As beautiful and emancipating as the aims or objectives of the Union and the principles for their workability appear to be, the implementation of those objectives has become a headache for analysts, even though there are divergent views in respect thereof. One of the objectives considered as being greatly neglected or not attended to with seriousness is that of promotion and protection of human and peoples' rights as contained in Article 3(h) of the Union's constitutive Act as well as the principle of intervention of the Union in member States in respect of grave circumstances such as "war crimes, genocide and crimes against humanity" as provided in Article 4(h) of the same Act. This occurred in Chad when the Chadian former President, Hissene Habre was indicted by Belgium, while acting under its extraterritorial legislation enacted in 2003, of allegedly being responsible for the killing of a large number of people and for even larger number of acts of torture, war crimes and human rights violations.[96] On the basis of the aforesaid indictment, Belgium asked Senegal (where he exiled himself to), to arrest and extradite Habre to Belgium. On 15th November, 2005 Senegal did arrest Habre, but the domestic court of competent jurisdiction ruled that it lacked jurisdiction to determine on his extradition to Belgium. In order alleviate itself from a potentially complicated situation, Senegal placed Habre at the disposal of the African Union and asked it to recommend the appropriate jurisdiction for his prosecution. Senegal did this in line with the provisions of Article 4(j) of the Union's Constitutive Act in order to restore peace and security in the country.

In January, 2006, the African Union Assembly decided to appoint a Committee of Eminent African Jurists with terms of reference to consider all aspects and implications of the case as well as to propose viable options for his trial.[97] The Eminent Jurists Committee submitted its report promptly to the Seventh Ordinary Session of the Assembly on 1st July, 2006. In the report, it recommended that Senegal should prosecute Habre in the "name of Africa" without explaining in detail what this novel proposition entailed.[98] Upon receiving the report, the Assembly considered that the Union lacked a legal organ to try Habre, and consequently mandated Senegal to prosecute him and to ensure that he received a fair trial.

In as much as the Assembly's pronouncement could be correct from a legal point of view, considering the non-existence of any judicial structure of the Union despite the provisions in the Constitutive Act for the Court of Justice,[99] it is submitted

---

96   Reports on International Organisations, op. cit.
97   See African Union (AU) Decision on the Hissene Habre case and the African Union Doc. Assembly/AU/Dec.(vi) January 24, 2006
98   See the Report of the Committee of Eminent African Jurists on the case of Hissene Habre, (July 1, 2006) available at http://www.africa-union.org/ Retrieved on 2/10/2010
99   See Article 5(1)(d) of the Constitutive Act

that the pronouncement smacks of the defence of a lazy person who has failed or omitted to perform his lawful duty despite having the resources at his disposal. One way the Union would have averted this "shameful" decision as to have constituted the African Court of Justice with the "Eminent African Jurists" readily available. In the alternative, the Union or one of its member States would have lodged complaints against Senegal since it refused to prosecute Habre, to African Commission on Human and Peoples Rights. Better still, the complaint would have been made at the African Court of Human and Peoples' Rights which in theory has become operative since 2004, but still remains inactive, as a test case for it. [100]

Senegal's failure to prosecute Habre was said to have been based on the problematic provision in its Constitution which prohibited the prosecution of crimes (including crimes committed against humanity) that were committed prior to the promulgation of the relevant legislation. This was in line with the principle of law that a crime can be said to have been committed only when a law provides for it.[101] In addition to that the Constitution also provided for limitation in prosecuting offences for ten years after which the alleged offence would not be prosecuted. This would have or had applied to Habre's case because the alleged crimes were committed between 1982 and 1990, therefore it was above the ten year-limitation period. Again, the Constitution prohibited the prosecution of crimes committed outside the country's territory. [102]

---

100 See the Report on African Union, regarding the African Court of Human and Peoples Rights (April 2, 2008) at http://.asil.org/rio/Africanunion-2008.html retrieved on 2/10/2010

101 This provision is also found in section 36(8) of the Constitution of the Federal Republic of Nigeria, 1999

102 See 2008 Report on AU op. cit.

Some commentators have argued that one way of viewing the case of the Chadian former President Hissene Habre is that it constitutes the first ever occasion that African Union has put into practice its right to intervene in a member State's internal affairs and has implemented the principle of condemning and rejecting impunity and political assassinations.[103] The argument is a total misconception of the position and it is not a correct approach. For the purpose of clarity as stated earlier, Habre was the former President of Chad, therefore, Habre's case should not be regarded as Senegal's internal affairs. Additionally, the Union did not interfere in the internal affairs of Senegal; it was only invited by Senegal to help solve the complicated situation. Even then, the Union referred the case back to Senegal, but with instruction or advise that he should be prosecuted in "the name of Africa" without even providing financial assistance in order to ascribe to it that it has implemented the principle of "condemning and rejecting impunity and political assassination" as argued above. It is apposite to state that Habre was a citizen of Chad, who fled to Senegal when his regime collapsed, and who was accused by Belgium of having committed torture and other acts that would probably qualify as crimes against humanity. Habre's case with Senegal is that he resided in its territory (for asylum) and, of course, Senegal tolerated his presence. It is submitted that given the transnational aspects that characterised the case of Habre and the stated inability of current African judicial and quasi-judicial institutions to deal with the case, the Union's Assembly would have created an *ad-hoc*

---

103 This argument was canvassed in "TOWARD A PEOPLE DRIVEN AFRICAN UNION: CURRENT OBSTACLES AND NEW OPPORTUNITIES," 44 African Network on Debt and Development, Open Society Initiative for Southern Africa and Oxfam GB, January 2007. Available at http://www.soros.org/resources/articlespublications/publications/people-124 retrieved on 2/10/2010.

judicial institution to handle the case. It is rather unfortunate that the Assembly did not have the idea of creating an ad-hoc internationalised regional criminal court, akin to those promoted by the United Nations in Sierra Leone, Cambodia and Lebanon. It is irresistibly unarguable that this would have created an excellent opportunity to generate a discussion on an array of issues that have been plaguing Africa, and probably proffer solution to the roots of gross violations of human rights; the tradition of non-prosecution of former and even serving leaders accused of heinous crimes; culture of impunity and political assassinations among others.

No wonder, even after the United Nations set an International Criminal Court of Justice to try President Omar Al-Bashir of Sudan for crimes against humanity, the Union at its 15th Ordinary Summit at Kampala, Uganda, refused to release Al-Bashir for trial to the Court, claiming that it envisaged unfair trial against Al-Bashir. This decision received wider condemnation particularly from the media arguing that African leaders were not serious with the acclaimed protection and promotion of Human and Peoples Rights.[104] It again confirms the preceding argument that the Union has been paying lip-service to the very important issue of human rights and even human life in contradistinction to the objectives and principles of the Union as contained in the Union's constitutive Act. This laxity applied to other areas such as health, promotion of economic cooperation, democracy and good governance. For instance, the current political impasse in Cote d'Ivoire has clearly demonstrated the Union's inability to fulfil the purpose for which it was created. On the 13th December, 2010, it was reported that "African Union does not favour sanctions, for now, over a disputed presidential

---

104 "Are African Leaders serious with the protection of Human Rights" the editorial of the Nation Newspapers, Thursday, 19th August, 2010, p.10

election in Ivory Coast and would stick to diplomacy."[105] This is a situation whereby one country has been running shamelessly, two parallel administrations on the account of Laurent Gbagbo's refusal to hand over power to the internationally recognised winner of the November 28, 2010 presidential election in that country. Meanwhile, the whole world including United Nations have recognised Alassane Ouattara as the winner of the election and he had been sworn in as the elected President of the country, but Mr. Gbagbo supported by the Constitutional Council (created by Laurent Gbagbo) and the country's army still cringed to power in the spirit of African leaders' politics of "do-or-die" affair. The decision of Mr. Gbagbo has made United Nations, European Union, France "the father" of the country, among others, to sanction Ivory Coast and Mr. Laurent Gbagbo as well as his allies. However, the African Union which would have taken urgent steps to avert "the shameful display" in the continent is happily considering other options to settle the crisis. It is again a clear indication that the Union has no regard to human life which is the basic fundamental right. This is because since the crisis started it has left hundreds of people dead, but the leaders are still on the fence. The situation in Cote d'Ivoire is an aberration of democratic tenets, and first of its kind in the history of modern democracy.

Another area where the Union has failed, or at least, is yet to achieve its objectives is terrorism. The menace of terrorism is the plague that has, in recent times, bedevilled the continent with no iota of hope to quell it. Many African countries including Nigeria, the giant of Africa, have witnessed one form of terrorism or the other. In Nigeria, for instance, the "October 1, 2010 twin-bomb blasts" in Abuja was the peak of terrorism

---

105   Ohia P.K. "AU: Talks Not Sanctions Best for Cote d'Ivoire" ThisDay Newspaper, Monday December 13, 2010 p.76

in the country coming at the time the country was celebrating her 50th anniversary. On this day, the whole world gathered in Abuja to rejoice with Nigeria during her Golden Jubilee celebration of freedom from colonial control. Some disgruntled elements "appreciated the visitors' presence" with bomb blasts. In some States such as Bauchi, Borno, Plateau, Bayelsa terrorism manifests itself in different forms such as Boko Haram, Jos crisis among others to the dismay and trauma of innocent citizens. The worst of terrorism occurred in Uganda when the whole world gathered in Africa for the first time to stage football world cup competition. This incident was widely condemned by analysts who described the acts as "condemnable".[106] It has been posited that:

> The bombings by Al-Shabab in Uganda are condemnable. Any indiscriminate violent attack on innocent citizens is cowardly immoral and evil, and has deviated from armed conflict to crime against humanity. It is even more unfortunate that they took place at the height of the glory of the continent when South Africa hosted the world to a football fiesta. [107]

Indeed, this was not a pat on the back of Africa and in particular African Union. Even in the face of this, the Union did not lend its voice in condemning the dastardly acts; and its action remains in the coffins. Apart from that, it has been argued that the present government in Somalia is so only in name, as it only controls a tiny part of the capital; an attempt to restore

---

106 See "Africa's Open Sore" an editorial of the Nation Newspaper, Thursday July 22, 2010, p.17

107 Ibid. This dastardly act does not spare security men, and military formations as Mogadishu Barracks in Abuja also witnessed bomb blast on the 31st December, 2010 as "End of year package" to the army.

peace in the country by African Union through peace-keeping force is in no way successful.[108] In both Uganda and Somalia, terrorist activities are on the increase even in the presence of African Union's Peace-keeping forces. This again shows that the proclamation by the Union to "respect sanctity of human life, condemnation and rejection of impunity and political assassination, acts of terrorism and subversive activities" as contained in Article 4(o) is in no way realistic.

Health, which has been considered to be very crucial and central in human existence is one of the areas where African Union is yet to fulfil its objectives. Despite the 2001 Abuja Declaration by the African leaders to commit 15% of their national budgets to health sector, the sector is still worst hit by neglect.[109] The realization remains a myth; and in recognition of their failure to fulfil the promise, the issue came up again at the 15th Ordinary Summit of the African Union in Kampala, Uganda in 2010. With the theme "Maternal, Infant and Child Health and Development in Africa", the thirty-five heads of State and Government, who attended the summit "pledged to recommit themselves to an earlier declaration in Abuja in 2001, wherein they would devote 15 percent of their national budgets to the health sector."[110] The leaders also pledged to strengthen their health systems, so as to provide comprehensive and integrated maternal, newborn and child care services. The question that remains unanswered or rhetoric is, to what extent would the leaders go with their "recommitment" pledge, considering the fact that in the past ten years they made similar pledge but did not fulfil it? It is submitted that unless and until the member States and

---

108 Ibid
109 Hamza S. "How Committed are African Leaders to Child, Maternal Health?" The Nation Newspaper, August 8, 2010, p.28
110 Ibid

their leaders turn away from the African mentality of speaking without backing the words up with action, the continent will witness devastating health implications, and efficacious consequences of the inaction.

From the above discourse, it is irresistibly unarguable that African Union has not lived up to its expectations. As beautiful as the "paper-objectives" and principles appear to be, if no urgent steps are taken by the member States, the hope of African citizens, which was renewed with the emergence of the Union, will be dashed to the rocks.

Organisation and Functions of the Union

The African Union, being a legal entity or personality, it is potently clear that it must possess organs like a natural being to effectively carry out its duties. To this end, after the process of formation of the Union, the Heads of States and Governments called for a summit at Lusaka to look at the implementation process of the Union. At the summit, the Secretary-General of the then Organisation of African Unity, was mandated to work out the modalities and guidelines for the launching of the Organs of the Union, including the preparation of the draft Rule of Procedure of such Organs, and to also ensure the effective exercising of authority and discharging of their responsibilities.[111] Most of the key organs of the African Union are established under the provisions of the African Union Constitutive Act.[112] However, some of the organs are set up under protocols to the Constitutive Act of the Union or those to the Abuja Treaty establishing African Economic Community, free-standing treaties as well as other legal documentation. [113]

---

111 Document for "Transition from the OAU to the African Union" op. cit. p.3
112 See Article 5(1) of the AU Constitutive Act
113 Some of these organs include New Partnership for Africa's Development (NEPAD), Peace and Security Council of the Union, etc.

It has been contended that during the process for the establishment of the organ of the African Union, the challenge faced was how to move away from overly state-centric character of the Organisation of African Unity and its concomitant lack of civil participation. During the Lusaka summit, several references were made to the African Union being loosely based on the European Union model, in which respect it was said that "Africa should not reinvent the wheel."[114] It was however, agreed that the African Union should be something new, with the emphasis on being African experience.[115] What however remains unclear is the statement "Africa should not re-invent". This could best be described as a house rat eating the foot of the owner but only blowing air to cushion the effect. There is no doubt that African Union is a replica of European Union. The use of the caveat after the founders of the Union significantly agreed to, and copied the European Union largely is tantamount to the biblical saying that the wicked runs where no one pursues him. It is submitted that the defence of the founders "not to re-invent the wheel" is a weak one, therefore it must collapse.

The wheel of the African Union otherwise known as the organs of the Union and their functions are considered hereunder.

The Assembly of the Union

The Assembly of the Union comprises the Heads of States and Governments of all the member States and is the highest decision-making body of the African Union. The assembly meets once in a year in ordinary session except in case of extraordinary session which may be convened by the chairperson of the Union or any member State with the consent of at least

114   See "Transition from the OAU to the African Union" op. cit. p.5
115   Ibid

two-thirds of the member States.[116] The Constitutive Act of the Union is very specific about the powers and functions of the Assembly as the supreme organ of the Union. Those powers are provided for under Article 9 of the Union's Constitutive Act. Article 9(1) provides that the functions of the Assembly shall be to: *determine the common policies of the Union; receive, consider and take decisions on reports and recommendations from other organs of the Union; consider request for membership of the Union; establish any organs of the Union; monitor the implementation of policies and decisions of the Union as well as ensure compliance by all member States; adopt the budget of the Union; give directions to the Executive Council on the management of conflict, war and other emergency situations and the restoration of peace. Other functions of the Assembly are to appoint the Chairman of the Commission and determine their functions and terms of office; and to appoint and terminate the appointment of Court of Justice members.*

The Assembly adopts decisions by majority votes. At most summits, the Assembly adopts two types of proposal, namely, decisions which are binding on member States according to their language; and declarations which are intended to guide and harmonise the viewpoints of member States but are not binding. It has been contended that the Assembly has the power to impose sanctions against any member State that fails to comply with decisions and policies as provided under Article 23 of the Union's Constitutive Act.[117] As stated earlier, the Assembly of the Union, which is composed of Heads of States and Governments or their duly accredited representatives, is the supreme organ of the Union.[118] This therefore, implies that the major

---

116   Chitiga R. op. cit. p.6
117   Chitiga R. op. cit. p.7
118   See Article (2) of the Union's Constitutive Act

policies and decisions of the Union in particular, and Africa, by extension are taken by the Assembly of the Union. That being the case, it has been rightly argued that the Assembly of the Union is the organ that decides on intervention as provided for under Article 4(h) of the Constitutive Act of the African Union in respect of war and crimes against humanity. The protocol on Amendments to the Constitutive Act has increased the number of situations wherein the Union may intervene in the affairs of a member State, upon the recommendations of the Security and Peace Council.[119] Such situations include serious threat to legitimate order or to restore peace and security to the member State of the Union.

The question that begs for answer, without any doubt is despite the available legal instruments empowering the Assembly of the Union to effectively function, what is really hindering the "supreme organ" of the Union from taking decisions that will impact positively on the African citizens? The situations in Comoros and Ivory Coast (Cote d'Ivoire) have clearly shown that the Assembly of the Union, even though has been accorded with the supreme status, is ineffective. This again shows that the Union itself is weak and cannot be the "emancipator" of the African continent because the organ or institution of the Union, which even the Constitutive Act has described as the "Supreme organ" is a toothless bulldog. If the strong man of the house has manifested his weakness, it is taken that the whole house is but a mere structure without any value attached thereto. This is why the Union in its about ten years of existence has failed to make any significant impact on the continent. In fact, the Ivorian drama wherein even the sub-regional organisation, Economic Community of West African States (ECOWAS), has

---

119 The Protocol was adopted in 2003 and it came into force in May, 2004 after the ratification by the two-thirds majority (27) of the member states.

aired out its decision, the African Union, which is the father of the continent, is only trying to join forces with the sub-regional body to end the impasse. It is incontrovertibly clear that the Union is not a solution to the emerging problems of the continent as "envisaged" by the founding fathers, some of whom are still in power. [120]

Considering the above discussions therefore, it is unarguably axiomatic that the Assembly of the Union which is said to be the supreme organ of the institution has not performed its functions as required. The only area wherein the Assembly is said to have "performed" is the establishment of other organs of the Union such as Peace and Security Council[121] and New Partnership for Africa's Development, otherwise called NEPAD as contained in Article 9(d) of the Constitutive Act. [122]

However, this could best be described as an administrative act with little or no stress. Even in the case of NEPAD, it was only an adoption of an already existing institution. Since the Assembly has performed below average, it is safer to conclude that the Union has not met the yearnings and aspirations of African citizens and as such much is not expected from the other less powerful organs of the Union.

The Executive Council

The Executive Council of African Union is regarded as a meeting of Ministers of Foreign Affairs of member States and such other ministers charged with the responsibility of dealing with the African Union matters as they relate to member

---

120 Colonel Muammar Gadhafi of Libya, the arrowhead of the Union's formation is still in power, but some analysts accuse him of being a stumbling block to the effective performance of the Union.

121 See the Protocol for the Amendment of the Constitutive Act, 2003

122 This was done at the 15th Ordinary Summit held at Kampala, Uganda in 2010

States.[123] This organ of the Union is creased by the Constitutive Act. Article 10(1) of the Act provides that "the Executive Council shall be composed of the ministers of Foreign Affairs or such other ministers or authorities as are designated for Governments of member States." The Council meets at least twice a year in ordinary session. Under Article 13(1) of the Union's Constitutive Act, the Executive Council has been empowered to coordinate and take decisions on policies in areas of common interest to member States. Such areas include foreign trade, energy, industry and mineral resources; food, agriculture and animal resources, livestock production and forestry; water resources and irrigation; environmental protection, humanitarian action and disaster response and relief; transport and communications; insurance, education, culture, health as well as human resources development. Other areas include science and technology; nationality, residence and immigration matters; social security, including the formulation of mother and child care policies as well as policies relating to the disabled and handicapped; and establishment of a system of African awards, models and prizes.

In furtherance of the above functions, the protocol for the Amendment of the Constitutive Act establishing Peace and Security Council, the Executive Council is also mandated to appoint the members of the Peace and Security Council, and also direct the Peace and Security Council to ensure that conflict prevention, management and resolution are achieved as and when due.[124] The Executive Council is also responsible for administrative and legal matters, including the elections of African Union officials, as delegated by the Assembly.[125] The per-

---

123 Transition from OAU to African Union op. cit. p.5
124 See the Protocol establishing Peace and Security Council, 2004
125 Chitiga R. op. cit. p.10

formance or otherwise of the Executive Council of the Union is dependent upon the performance of the Assembly of the Union. This is because by the provisions of Article 13(2) of the Union's Constitutive Act, "the Executive Council shall be responsible to the Assembly" and it only considers issues referred to it by the Assembly.

From the provisions of the Constitutive Act, which is the ground norm of the Union, the Executive Council cannot perform magic where the "supreme organ", the Assembly of the Union, fails to live up to expectations. It has been argued that since 2003, the Executive Council has been delegated by the Assembly to debate and approve the active reports of the African Commission on Human and People's Rights and African Court on Human and People's Rights, before they are published.[126] This argument or assertion is not patent that it has not increased any impact on the citizenry. This could be as a result of the failure of the Assembly to refer those functions the Act has empowered it to perform for it to carry out. It is submitted that the barrier placed against the free performance of the Executive Council by making it subordinate to Assembly is tantamount to giving the Council the duties with the right hand but using the left hand to collect them. It is further submitted that in order to enhance the performance of the Executive, it should be allowed to perform freely without any encumbrance. As it is now, failure of the Assembly automatically affects the performance of the Council, which is not in the best interest of the continent.

Pan-African Parliament

In order to ensure the full participation of African peoples in the development and economic integration of the continent,

---

126 ibid

the Pan-African Parliament was established or adopted by the Union through its Constitutive Act.[127] The Pan-African Parliament is recognised as one of the organs of the African Union under its Constitutive Act, though its detailed legal basis is said to be a protocol to the 1991 Abuja Treaty which established African Economic Community.[128] The protocol establishing Pan-African Parliament was adopted in 2000 during the organisation of African Unity Summit in Lome, Togo wherein the Union's Constitutive Act was adopted thereby making it an integral part of the Union. The parliament holds its regular sessions in March and November each year.

According to the protocol, Pan-African Parliament is expected to exercise advisory and consultative functions. These functions are to be reviewed after five years of its existence, with a view to giving it stronger powers, including passing legislation. In January, 2009, the Pan-African Parliament authorized African Union Commission to initiate the review of the functions in line with the protocol. It has been asserted that the Pan-African Parliament would perform only the advisory and consultative functions in the first five years.[129] From the above position, since the parliament empanelled the African Union Commission only in January, 2009, to carry out the review but the report is yet to be submitted, it is submitted that the Pan-African Parliament is in coma. Until revived by the review, even the said advisory and consultative functions cannot be performed by the Parliament. This reaffirms how inactive the Union is, instead of being proactive.

The Pan-African Parliament reports to the Assembly of the Union being the supreme organ and its budget is processed

---

127 See Article 17(1) of the Union's Constitutive Act
128 Chitiga R. op. cit. p.21
129 Ibid

through the policy organs of the African Union.[130] The parliament is presided over by the Bureau headed by a chairperson and four vice chairpersons. It has ten permanent committees responsible for thematic issues and the management of the parliament's business.[131] Each of the member states of the African Union that ratified the Pan-African Parliament's protocol is entitled to five representatives to its meetings, selected from national parliaments or other deliberative bodies, at least one of whom must be a woman.

Since the Parliament has only the advisory and consultative functions to perform in the first five years, much is not expected from it. By implication, it seems the parliament only acts on those issues referred to it for advice or consultation. This therefore, means that even if the parliament performs its functions, they may not be visibly seen, who performs, but to the credit of the masquerade. It is therefore, submitted that, if the functions of the parliament are to be reviewed as contained in the protocol, the parliament should be given specific functions for the progress of the continent. It may be made the legislative organ of the Union, subject to the Assembly of the Union.

The Court of Justice

In order to ensure that the Constitutive Act of the Union and other instruments regulating the Union's activities and those of its organs are not mere expressions, the Constitutive Act of the Union has provided for the establishment of the Court of Justice otherwise called African Court of Justice. The Constitutive Act provides under Article 18 that, "A Court of Justice of the Union shall be established; and the status, composition and

---

130 Such organs include New Partnership for Africa's Development (NEPAD), African Peer Review Mechanism (APRM) among others.
131 Chitiga R. op. cit. p.21

functions of the Court of Justice shall be defined in a protocol relating thereto.[132] By the provisions of the Act, the functions, composition and powers of the Court would be elaborated upon in a protocol, which classify what the impact of the Court on domestic legislations will be.

Some scholars have asserted that the Constitutive Act provides for a Court of Justice to rule on the disputes over interpretation of the Union's treaties.[133] In compliance with the provisions of the Constitutive Act to bring the Court into existence, a protocol is to set it forth. In a bid to strengthen the African justice system, a decision was taken at the 2004 Ordinary Summit of the Union to merge the African Court of Justice and African Court of Human and Peoples' Rights whose protocol came into force in the same year, 2004.[134] The purpose of merging them was to establish a combined or single court known as African Court of Justice and Human Rights. In July 2008, African Heads of State finally adopted the protocol on the statute of the African Court of Justice and Human Rights, which when it commences operation will supersede the two existing protocols establishing the courts. The merged Court, which will have its headquarters in Arusha, will have two chambers, for human rights and general matters. The new protocol will come into effect once 15 states have ratified it; in the meantime, the African Court of Human and Peoples' Rights remains in place. [135]

It has been posited that the Court of Justice and Human Rights, when established, will have authority to judge disputes about the Constitutive Act and the other protocols and treaties adopted by the African Union or its predecessor, Organisation

---

132   See Article 18(1) and (2) of the Act
133   Chitiga R. op. cit. p.25
134   Ibid
135   Ibid

of African Unity, including the African Charter on Human and Peoples' Rights and its protocols.[136] Cases can be referred to the Court by the Union's member states that have ratified the protocol, by the African Commission on Human and Peoples' Rights, by the Assembly and the African Union Commission.[137] What however, remains worrisome is that ordinary or private citizens and Non-Governmental Organisations (NGOs) do not have the right of direct access to the existing Court of Human and Peoples' Rights or the merged Court.[138] It is submitted that the ouster provision contained in the protocol to the statute on the African Court of Justice and Human Rights is anti-the masses, therefore, it should be nipped in the bud. The situation whereby the common man whose hope is the judiciary is denied access to a "Court of Justice" is like the proverbial toad who, it is said, cannot live in the water when it is boiling, even though it likes water. When a toad is separated from the water, the expected result will inevitably be death, and that applies to a common man when he does not have access to justice. It is submitted further that the drafters of the protocol on the merged Court should have a second look at the outer provision by allowing private individuals and Non-Governmental Organisations which are watchdogs the access to the new Court in the interest of justice. This will revive and restore the hope of a common man in the African justice system.

In order to expand the jurisdictional "tentacles" of the court, even though it has not started operation, the Assembly of the Union decided to consider the possibility of empowering the court to try persons accused of international crimes or crimes

---

136   Ibid
137   Ibid
138   Ibid

against humanity.[139] This could best be described as empowering or giving responsibility to a foetus in the uterus without knowing whether it will be born alive or as a still born. In any event, if the Assembly wants the protocol amended for the purpose of additional jurisdiction, the Union will do that after the protocol might have come into force since some member states have started ratifying it. The intention of the Union is a welcome development because if the court is empowered to try those accused of crimes against humanity, it will prevent repetition of what transpired between Senegal and the Union in the case of Hissene Habre, the former President of Chad who took refuge in Senegal.[140]

The Union's Legal Order and Member States

An international institution having legal personality, it has the power to make orders regarding the co-existence of its member States. The legal order is to maintain orderliness, law and order in the entity. The legal order may be provided in the constituent instrument and/or decisions of such institutions or its organs having authority to make binding orders or decisions like courts.

Some commentators have posited that the enforcement of a treaty is safeguarded by political, economic and legal means.[141] The most important weapon, which in classic international law states may resort to in order to frustrate its enforcement is the interpretation of the treaty in relation to the concept of sovereignty. In some treaties however, such vertigo of sovereignty

139 See the preceding discussions
140 Ibid
141 Lasok D. and Bridge J.W. An Introduction to Law and Institutions European Community, 2nd edn (London: Butterworths Publishers Co., 1976) p.217

is taken away by the provisions of a constituent instrument.[142] Article 23 of the Constitutive Act of African Union has equally provided for imposition of sanctions on member States which fail to comply with the Union's legal order. Article 23(2) provides that:

> *Article 23(2) furthermore, any member state that fails to comply with the decisions and policies of the Union may be subjected to other sanctions, such as the denial of transport and communications links with other member states, and other measures of political and economic nature to be determined by the Assembly.*

From the above provisions of the Constitutive Act of the African Union, if any member state fails to comply with the decisions and policies of the African Union, the Union through the Assembly can impose sanctions under Article 23 of the Constitutive Act, including not only denial of the right to speak and vote at meetings, but also measures of political and economic nature. [143]

The workability of the beautiful provisions of Article 23 of the African Union's Constitutive Act remains a subject of controversy as some scholars have seen it as a bulldog armed to the teeth with little or no impact.[144] This argument stems from the position of the Union in relation to the case of the former President of Chad, Hissene Habre who exiled to Senegal after he was accused of crimes against humanity, torture, war crimes and

142 Lasok D. and Bridge J.W. An Introduction to Law and Institutions of European Community, 2nd edn (London: Butterworths Publishers Co., 1976) p.217

143 Chitiga R. op. cit. p.7

144 Magliveras K.D. "The African Union" in American Society of International Law Journal (2010) p.2 downloaded from http://www.africa-union.org/ on 2/10/2010

other human rights violations by Belgium. On the basis of the accusations or indictment by Belgium however, the competent court in Senegal ruled that it lacked jurisdiction to determine his extradition to Belgium.[145] However, in order to alleviate itself from a potentially complicated situation, a fortnight later, Senegal placed Habre at the disposal of the African Union and asked it to recommend the appropriate jurisdiction to prosecute him. In order to tackle the case at hand, the Assembly of the African Union decided to appoint a committee of Eminent Jurists in January, 2006. This Eminent Jurists Committee submitted its report promptly at the seventh ordinary Assembly Session in July, 2006 wherein it was recommended that Senegal should prosecute Habre in "the name of Africa."[146] Nevertheless, in the event, Senegal did nothing to implement the decision issued by the Assembly, which repeated the mandate at the January, 2007 session. Even after the re-mandate, Senegal did not commence proceedings against Habre but the Assembly, which is said to be the supreme organ of the Union, did not discuss the non-compliance during its July 2007 and January/February 2008 sessions.

The case of Habre, which was a litmus test for the African Union coupled with its inaction or non-reaction to Senegal's disobedience to the decision of the Assembly, portrayed it as a powerless institution, which is unable to confront complex situations to assail those member states that do not comply with its decisions and policies. Even though Senegal always maintained that internal constitutional constraints prevented it from trying or prosecuting offences or crimes that were not committed prior

---

145   Brody R. "The prosecution of Hissene Habre African Pinochet" 35 ENG. L. REV. 321 (2001) cited Magliveras Ibid

146   See African Union Report of the Committee of Eminent African Jurists on the case of Hissene Habre, (July 1, 2006) on http://www.africa-union.org/ retrieved on 2/10/2010

to the enactment of the relevant legislation; stipulated a ten-year statute of limitations (which would have allowed the prosecution of Habre to collapse) and barred prosecution of crimes committed outside its territory, Senegal had international commitment which it ought to have obeyed. By the international law principle of *pact sunt servanda*, which means that states are bound by the obligations in a treaty they are parties to, Senegal would have complied with the Union's order or decision irrespective of its internal constitutional constraints. This again, brings to question the ability of the Union to enforce its orders and policies even when a member state fails to comply with them in contradistinction to the beautiful provisions of Article 23 of the Union's Constitutive Act.

The recent case of Laurent Gbagbo in Cote d'Voire has clearly shown that the Union is inactive and cannot enforce its policies and decisions. In its bid to promote good governance and democracy, the African Union's Assembly adopted charter on Democracy, Elections and Governance at its 8th ordinary session in January 2007. By the provisions of Article 23 of the African charter on Democracy, Elections and Governance, "illegal means of accessing or maintaining power constitute an unconstitutional change of government." Article 23 defines unconstitutional change of government to include inter alia, "the refusal of an incumbent to surrender power after a free, fair and regular election." As elaborate as the provision is, the African Union with its interventionist power as provided under Article 4(h) of the Constitutive Act is watching the drama in Cote d'Ivoire with its arms akimbo. This practically shows that the Union's legal order is but a mere expression on paper without being backed up with actions. It is therefore submitted that, if the African Union would live up to expectations of Africans, it should be proactive, but if an event occurs before taking action, it should not be indolent in reacting to it. This is the only way African citizens can feel the impact of the Union's activities.

The Commission of African Union

The Commission of African Union is one of the sensitive organs of the Union and could best be regarded as the conduit through which the "government" of the Union performs. The Commission through its portfolio commissioners manages the day-to-day task of the Union and implements the policies of the African Union. The Constitutive Act of the Union provides under Article 20 that "there shall be established a Commission of the Union, which shall be the secretariat of the Union." This means that every activity or function of the Union must be known by the Commission since it is the "secretariat" of the Union. For effective and efficient performance of the Commission, the Commission is composed of the chairperson, his/her deputy or deputies and commissioners who are assisted by the necessary staff as determined by the Assembly of the Union.[147] At present, there are eight commissioners, who manage day-to-day tasks of the African Union in relation to their portfolios, and these officials hold office for concurrent five years.[148] The chairperson of the Union's Commission reports to the Executive Council of Ministers.

Historically, since the Organisation of African Unity (OAU) was founded there has been a debate among member states of the African Union over the framework for continental institutions and the balance between political and economic integration and national sovereignty. The early drive for a Union Government for Africa led by the then President of Ghana, Kwame Nkrumah, was defeated at the 1965 Accra summit of

---

147   See Article 20(2) and (3) of the Union's Constitutive Act
148   Chitiga R. op. cit. p.14

the Organisation, and a quarter century later, the 1991 Abuja Treaty establishing African Economic Community endorsed a "gradualist approach", creating a distant time table for the achievement of full integration. However, member states and some African citizens continued to lobby for a speedy integration to progress rapidly.[149] These debates led to the establishment of African Union and the debates have intensified.

It has been argued that pressure for more integrationist legal framework for the Union led to the appointment of a Committee of Seven Heads of State, who presented a report to the July 2006 Summit at Banjul.[150] The Union Commission was then mandated to produce a more detailed report on the issues, and produce a study on Union Government. This report was presented at the Addis Ababa Summit in January, 2007, to the Assembly of the Union. The Assembly then discussed the issue of Union Government at the Accra Summit on 1st – 3rd July, 2007. A panel of eminent persons was appointed to conduct the Audits Review and present a long and detailed report to the 2008 Summit on the functioning of the existing organs of the African Union. At January and July, 2008, Summits, the Assembly decided to postpone decision once again, however, the election of the chairperson and commissioners of the African Union Commission went ahead in January 2008 according to the previous system. The Assembly appointed a Committee of Twelve Heads of State and Government of Botswana, Cameroon, Egypt, Ethiopia, Gabon, Ghana, Libya, Nigeria, Senegal, South Africa, Tanzania and Uganda to review proposals made by the Audit Review Committee. At the July, 2008, Summit, the Assembly requested the African Union Commission to present a report on the modalities for implementing the recommendations

---

149   Ibid p.75
150   Ibid

of the "Committee of Twelve" to the February, 2009 Assembly, with a view to bringing the debate to a final conclusion at that meeting. At a special session of the Assembly held on 1st February, 2009, however, the Assembly decided to transform the African Union Commission into an authority, with strengthened resources and powers, and to refer further decisions once again to the next summit after further study of the necessary amendments to the Constitutive Act by an extra-ordinary session of the Executive Council.

The Executive Council met in Libya in April, 2009 to consider the functions of the new African Union's authority, the size of the authority, the functions of the secretaries who would lead the new departments and the implication of establishing the authority. The conclusions of the Executive Council's extra-ordinary session were modest. The Ministers endorsed the expansion of the areas of competence of the Union's authority, which will replace the Commission, but left the structure of the authority mostly unchanged from that of the Commission and did not follow the recommendations of the Audit Review to strengthen the chairperson. Despite the elevation of the Commission of the Union to the status of the "Authority of the Union", the Assembly of the Union still retains the right to delegate any function and/or power to any organ of the Union including the authority.[151] The authority has, however, been given the role to coordinate the Union position on key issues. These conclusions were endorsed by the Assembly during the June-July 2009 Summit, also held in Libya.

One issue that remains sacrosanct is that since the commission, the Authority is the engine as well as the fulcrum of the African Union, in spite of the retention of the power to del-

---

151   Ibid p.75

egate by the Assembly. The "Supreme Organ" Assembly of the Union, remains so only in theory without any practical impact. It is submitted that since the Assembly of the Union could not perform credibly in the past decade of the Union's existence the Authority of the Union with its expanded functions and powers should wake up to the clarion call by the African citizens for a better Africa. However, since the powers and functions of the Authority so expanded have not been clearly spelt out, it still remains a concern as to how the Authority will perform to the satisfaction of the citizenry. It is further submitted that the earlier those functions are clearly spelt out, the better for the continent.

Permanent Representatives Committee

The Permanent Representatives Committee is one of the organs of African Union established by the Constitutive Act of the Union. Article 21 of the Constitutive Act provides that there shall be established a Permanent Representatives Committee; and it shall be composed of permanent representatives to the Union and other plenipotentiaries of member states.[152] The Permanent Representatives Committee is charged with the responsibility of preparing the work of the Executive Council and acting on the Executive Council's instructions.

The Permanent Representatives Committee which is made of Ambassadors, representatives of member states also has the duty or oversight of day-to-day running of the commission now known as the Authority of the Union. It has been regarded as one of the most influential organs of the Union, and it meets once in a month.[153] The Permanent Representatives Committee also has the mandate to work closely with the

---

152   Ibid p.58
153   See Article 21(1) of the Constitutive Act

Union's Authority to implement the Union's programmes and to monitor the implementation of decisions reached at summits. According to the Committee's rules of procedure, any member state, African Union's organs or Regional Economic community may propose agenda for the Committee's meetings.[154] The Committee's powers and functions fall in four areas: liaison between member states and the Union's commission or Authority; oversight over commission or Authority as discussed above; support to the Executive Council in executing its powers and functions; and assisting the preparation of the Union's programme of activities.

The Committee also has optional responsibility of setting up sub-committees or working groups as it may deem necessary.[155] The sub-committees will discuss technical and administrative questions as delegated by the Permanent Representatives Committee. The Committee has set up the following sub-committees: Advisory sub-committee on administrative, budgetary and financial matters; sub-committee on programmes and conferences; sub-committee on refugees; sub-committee on contributions; policy sub-committee of the special Emergency Assistance Fund for Drought and Famine in Africa; sub-committee on structural reforms; sub-committee on headquarters and host agreements; sub-committee on economic and trade matters; and sub-committee on multilateral cooperation. These sub-committees are to assist the Permanent Representatives Committee in attaining its set goals for the good of African continent. Since this organ of the Union meets more frequent than any other, it is submitted that the committee should be given the day-to-day administration of the Union. This is because the plenipotentiaries are the eyes of the member states; therefore,

---

154   Chitiga R. op. cit. p.12
155   Ibid

any decision taken by the committee will involve all the member states. If the committee's functions and powers are expanded and strengthened, it will be more proactive than the Assembly of the Union.

Specialised Technical Committees

The Constitutive Act of the African Union created the specialised Technical Committees which would be established at the Headquarters of the Union in Addis Ababa, Ethiopia. The specialised Technical Committees, when established, shall be responsible to the Executive Council of the Union.[156] Article 14(1) (a)-(g) enumerated seven technical committees to be established in the Union, and such include:

(a) *The Committee on Rural Economy and Agricultural matters;*

(b) *The Committee on Monetary and Financial Affairs;*

(c) *The Committee on Trade, Customs and immigration matters;*

(d) *The Committee on Industry, Science and Technology, Energy, Natural Resources and Environment;*

(e) *The Committee on Transport, Communications and Tourism;*

(f) *The Committee on Health, Labour and Social Affairs; and*

(g) *The Committee on Education, Culture and Human Resources.*

---

156   Article 21(2) of the Constitutive Act of the Union

The specialised Technical Committees shall be composed of ministers or senior officials responsible for sectors falling within the competence of the respective committees.

The Assembly of the Union has the responsibility to whenever it deems appropriate, restructure the existing committees or establish other committees.[157] The committees have been mandated to prepare projects and programmes of the Union and submit to the Executive Council; ensure the coordination and harmonisation of projects and programmes of the Union; submit to the Executive Council, either on its own initiative or at the request of Executive Council, reports and recommendations on the implementations.

Since the creation of African Union, the specialized of the provisions the Constitutive Act of the Union; and carry out any other functions assigned to it for the purpose of ensuring the implementation of the provisions of the Union's Constitutive Act.[158] Technical Committees had not been created until in January, 2009 when the Assembly of the Union decided to configure the committees into a set of 14 rather than the seven proposed by the Constitutive Act.[159]

The action of the Assembly was in line with the mandate given to the Assembly by the Union's Constitutive Act as provided under Article 14(2). The 14 committees created by the Assembly in 2009 include: The committee on Rural Economy; the committee on Agricultural matters; the committee on Monetary and Financial Affairs; the committee on Trade; the committee on Customs and Immigration matters; the committee on Industry; the committee on Science, Technology and Energy; the committee on Natural Resources and Environment; the commit-

---

157 See Article 14(1) of the Constitutive Act
158 See Article 14(2) and (3) of the Constitutive Act of the African Union
159 See Article 14(2) and (3) of the Constitutive Act of the African Union

tee on Transport and Communications; the committee on Tourism; the committee on Health, the committee on Labour and Social Affairs; the committee on Education; and the committee on Cultural and Human Resources. However, since the committees were restructured by the Assembly, there is no visible or tangible function performed by them. This is evident in area such as Agriculture; Transport and Communications; Science and Technology among others wherein the member states are lagging behind. The failure of the committees could be greatly attributed to the ineptitude on the part of the Assembly of the Union which failed to constitute the committees since the formation of the Union. The question that begs for answers but without any is which organ was responsible for the functions of the specialised Technical Committees since the formation of the Union? Being the creations of the constituent instrument of the Union, they ought to have taken off alongside other organs but for the laxity of the "Supreme Organ" of the Union, which is like an entity of its own. It is however, submitted that the committees should wake up to their responsibilities in the interest of the continent.

CHAPTER FOUR

Formation of Common Economic Policy

"Common territory, language and culture may in fact be present in a nation, but the existence of a nation does not necessarily imply the presence of all three. Common territory and language alone may form the basis of a nation. Similarly, common territory plus common culture may be the basis. In some cases, only one of the three applies. A state may exist on a multi-national basis. The community of economic life is the major feature within a nation, and it is the economy which holds together the people living in a territory. It is on this basis that the new Africans recognise themselves as potentially one nation, whose domination is the entire African continent." *Class Struggle in Africa-Kwame Nkrumah.*

T he objectives behind the formation of African Union by some selected African leaders was in line with the philosophy of the formation of European Union in the 1950s towards addressing political and economic issues. However, the level of progress that the European Union had made over the years cannot put to question the readiness of African leaders to truly use the AU in addressing the existing political and economic challenges facing the continent. For the fact that putting in place basic institutional framework like the establish-

ment of the New Partnership for Africa's Development (NEPAD) came belatedly underscore the lack of preparedness of the African leaders in tackling developmental challenges like their European counterparts. However, since process of nation building is rather of a project in progress, it is expected that greater progress can still be recorded in the near future when dynamic and visionary leaders eventually emerge.

The Financial Institutions

In line with the African Union's objective on promotion of sustainable development in African economy as provided under Article 3(j) of the Union's Constitutive Act, Article 19 provides for three financial institutions which will serve as a catalyst for the attainment of the objectives. The three financial institutions are: African Central Bank, African Monetary Fund and African Investment Bank. Even though these financial institutions are very vital to the achievement of the Union's objectives, they have remained unattended to as little or no attention has been paid to them. In fact, of the three institutions, only African Investment Bank that its statutes were formally adopted at the June, 2009 Summit of the African Union and the Protocol establishing the Bank was opened for ratification by member states.[160] However, the protocol has not come into force because the number of the member states required to ratify it to come into force has not been met. It is submitted that since the economy of every nation state or continent is dependent upon the available financial institutions, it is critical that member states should ratify the protocol so as to bring the African Investment Bank into existence. The African Central Bank's steering committee which was recently set up by the Assembly of the Union to mobilise the

---

160 Ibid

resources for its take-off should expedite action in order to bring it into operation for the development of the continent. If these financial institutions come into operation, the issue of contribution from member states for the Union's activities will be greatly reduced thereby accelerating its performance.

The Peace and Security Council

The Peace and Security Council was not part of the organs of the African Union which were originally created by the Union's Constitutive Act as contained in Article 5(i). However, the provisions of Articles 5(2) and 9(1)(d) of the Constitutive Act, the Assembly of Union has the power to establish any other organ of the Union with a view to attaining the Union's objectives. In view of the above provisions, the Peace and Security Council (otherwise called PSC) was established as an organ of the African Union under a Protocol to the Constitutive Act adopted by the African Union's Assembly in July 2002. The Protocol in Article 5(2) defines the Peace and Security Council as a collective security and early warning arrangement to facilitate timely and effective response to the conflict and crisis situations in Africa. The Peace and Security Council Protocol came into force on 26th December, 2003, after ratification by 27 of the 53 African Union Members, and the Council officially began its work on the 16th March, 2004 at the ministerial level, at the margins of the 4th Ordinary Session of the Union's Executive Council. It has been argued that Peace and Security Council is a decision-making body in its own right, and it takes initiatives and actions as it deems fit and its decisions are binding on member states of the Union.[161] The question that remains unanswered is how binding are the Peace and Security Council's decisions and how

---

161   Chitiga R. op. cit. p.34

are the Union's member states obedient to the decisions of the Council? This question will be tackled best in the course of this discourse.

The Peace and Security Council is said to have the power, among other things, to authorise peace missions, to impose sanctions in case of unconstitutional change of government and to take initiatives and actions it deems appropriate in response to potential or actual conflict. Article 4 of the Union's Constitutive Act repeated in Article 4 of the PSC protocol, recognizes the right of the Union to intervene in a member state in case of war crimes, genocide and crimes against humanity. Any decision to intervene in a member state under Article 4 of the Constitutive Act will be made by the Assembly on the recommendation of the Peace and Security Council. The Peace and Security Council is also responsible for implementation of the Non-aggression and Common Defence Pact adopted in 2005 (though it has not come into force yet) among whose commitments are that state parties undertake to prohibit and prevent genocide, other forms of mass murders as well as crimes against humanity. It has been argued in favour of the Council that since its first meeting in 2004, it has been "active in relation to the crisis in Darfur, Comoros, Somalia, Democratic Republic of Congo, Burundi, Cote de'Ivoire and other countries."[162] This argument is far from holding water. As rightly argued, even though mildly:

> In practice, the PSC has devoted relatively little attention to the prevention of conflict or addressing structural issues that encourage "bad governance". As one PSC official put it, ultimately, the organisation needs to decide whether it wants to focus on developing a more efficient fire service or building

---

162 Ibid

> *better, fire-proof houses. To date, the Council has*
> *clearly, opted to act as a fire extinguisher, dealing*
> *only with issues after they erupt... it seems that*
> *in order for a country to make it unto the Council's*
> *agenda it needed to witness the emergence of an*
> *open rebellion or serious insurgency."* [163]

This argument is true and therefore cannot be faulted in any way. For instance, despite the suffering caused by Robert Mugabe's regime, no attempt was made to put Zimbabwe on the Peace and Security Council's agenda. The response of the Council to the violent aftermath of the Kenya's elections in December, 2007 wherein many Kenyan citizens were killed is another example. The Council with the sword of sanction in its hand did not slam it on the perpetrators of the heinous act thereby encouraging violence. The situation in Cote d'Ivoire is a clear indication that the Council is a toothless bulldog who can only bark but cannot bite. In Cote d'Ivoire, the defeated President Laurent Gbagbo who still sticks to power despite the declaration of his challenger in the November, 2010 Presidential election as the winner is comfortably enjoying the support of the state security apparatus at the expense of the internationally recognized winner of the said election, but the Council has not taken any action to restore the constitutional government as it claims to have such mandate.

By Article 20 of the Peace and Security Council's Protocol, the Council is to encourage civil society organisations to participate actively in the efforts aimed at promoting peace and security in Africa. In furtherance of the mandate, in December, 2008 the Council adopted a document setting out the mo-

---

163 Ibid

dalities for interacting civil society organisations known as the "Livingstone formula". In line with the said document, the civil society organisations from both Kenya and Zimbabwe did brief members of the Peace and Security Council on the situation in their respective countries but there was no positive response from the Council.[164] This has practically justified the argument that the Council has not lived up to its mandate. The recent position of the Council on the Cote d'Ivoirian crisis reaffirms unequivocally the above argument. It is submitted that in order to achieve the Union's objective of good governance and democracy in its member states, the Peace and Security Council should wake up from its slumber to face the challenges staring in its face. Without peace, there will be no meaningful economic growth in the continent.

The New Partnership for African Development (NEPAD)

The New Partnership for African Development (NEPAD) is an economic development programme of the African Union. NEPAD was adopted at the 37th session of the Assembly of Heads of State and Government in July 2001 in Lusaka, Zambia. NEPAD aims to provide an overarching vision and policy framework for accelerating economic co-operation and integration among African countries.

The New Partnership for African Development (NEPAD) is said to be the strategic framework setting out a vision for Africa's renewal. Its founding document was formally adopted by the 37th Summit of the Organization of African Unity (OAU) in Lusaka, Zambia in 2001. Since the Union inherited almost

---

164   William P.D. "The Peace and Security Council of the African Union: Evaluating an Embryonic International Institution" The paper presented to the panel "Do International Institutions have future in International Security?" At ISA Annual Convention, San Francisco, 26-30 March, 2008 p.5

all the structures of the Organisation of African Unity, NEPAD became a programme of the African Union with its secretariat in South Africa to coordinate implementation of its economic programmes.[165] The NEPAD document was endorsed for the first time by the African Union at its first Summit in Durban in 2002. However, NEPAD became the Union's structure or organ finally in July 2010 when its Protocol was adopted by the Union's Assembly at its 15th Ordinary Summit in Kampala, Uganda.

The New Partnership for Africa's Development's secretariat, which is based in Midrand, South Africa, reports to the NEPAD Heads of State and Government Implementation Committee (HSGIC) which usually in the margins of the African Union Summits and in turn reports to the Union's Assembly.[166] Its activities are funded by voluntary contributions from member States of the African Union. NEPAD, as a programme of the African Union and very recently, an organ of the Union, therefore, places premium on establishing a more vibrant global partnership and relationship to drive Africa's sustainable development, with a new structured approach to resources mobilisation aimed at reducing chronic finance gap per annum. The advanced industrialised countries of G8 as well as regional and multilateral development institutions are said to have become integral partners in the process of constructing this partnership.[167]

It has been posited that at the 12th Summit of the 2005 Algiers NEPAD Heads of State and Governments Implementation Committee (HSGIC) Summit, African leaders identified five

---

165 The Inability of the Peace and Security Council to stage-manage the Crisis in Sudan led to referendum for the cessation of the Southern Sudan in 2011 as an independent state from the North

166 "African Peer Review Mechanism: A Compilation of Studies of the Process in Nine African Countries", a document of an Open Society Foundation Publication, 2009 downloaded from www.compressdsl. On 28th December, 2010

167 Chitiga R. op. cit. p.29

priority areas that would form the basis for the speedy implementation of New Partnership for Africa's development policies.[168] Consequently, at the 13th Summit of the Heads of State and Government Implementation Committee held in Sham-el-Sheikh, Egypt, the priorities were reaffirmed to form the basis of the engagement with G8 Summit held in Gleneagles, United Kingdom. The same priorities were then endorsed by 5th African Union Heads of State and Government Summit in July, 2005 in Libya. The G8 leaders on their part signalled their political and economic support for Africa, largely in line with what African leaders had called for. Consequently, a consultative process involving African Ministers of Finance, African Union Commission/New Partnerships for Africa's Development Secretariat, Regional Economic (RECs), Country experts and partner institutions experts was undertaken to come out with an all-embracing but concise Action plan.[169] The African Action Plan is an initiative that wholly embodies the NEPAD principles of African ownership and responsibility; commitment to good political, economic and corporate governance; self-reliance, people-centred development; gender equality; promotion of action-oriented partnership with stakeholders within Africa and with the international community, and leadership.[170]

NEPAD is a merger of two plans for the economic regeneration of Africa: the Millennium Partnership for the African Recovery Programme (MAP), led by Former President Thabo Mbeki of South Africa in conjunction with Former President Olusegun Obasanjo of Nigeria and President Abdelaziz Bouteflika of Algeria; and the OMEGA Plan for Africa developed by President

---

168 See 10th African Partnership Forum (APF) held in Tokyo, Japan on 7th – 8th April, 2000 "AU/NEPAD AFRICAN ACTION" p.2
169 Ibid
170 Ibid p.3

Abdoulaye Wade of Senegal. At a summit in Sirte, Libya, March 2001, the Organisation of African Unity (OAU) agreed that the MAP and OMEGA Plans should be merged.[1]

The UN Economic Commission for Africa (UNECA) developed a "Compact for Africa's Recovery" based on both these plans and on resolutions on Africa adopted by the United Nations Millennium Summit in September 2000, and submitted a merged document to the Conference of African Ministers of Finance and Ministers of Development and Planning in Algiers, May 2001.[2]

July, 2001, the OAU Assembly of Heads of State and Government meeting in Lusaka, Zambia, adopted this document under the name of the New African Initiative (NAI). The leaders of G8 countries endorsed the plan on July 20, 2001; and other international development partners, including the European Union, China, and Japan also made public statements indicating their support for the programme. The Heads of State and Government Implementation Committee (HSGIC) for the project finalised the policy framework and named it the New Partnership for Africa's Development on 23 October, 2001. NEPAD is now a program of the African Union (AU) that has replaced the OAU in 2002, though it has its own secretariat based in South Africa to coordinate and implement its programmes.

NEPAD's four primary objectives are: to eradicate poverty, promote sustainable growth and development, integrate Africa in the world economy, and accelerate the empowerment of women. It is based on underlying principles of a commitment to good governance, democracy, human rights and conflict resolution; and the recognition that maintenance of these standards is fundamental to the creation of an environment conducive to investment and long-term economic growth. NEPAD seeks to attract increased investment, capital flows and funding, providing an African-owned framework for development as the foundation for partnership at regional and international levels.

In July, 2002, the Durban AU summit supplemented NEPAD with a Declaration on Democracy, Political, Economic and Corporate Governance. According to the Declaration, states participating in NEPAD 'believe in just, honest, transparent, accountable and participatory government and probity in public life'. Accordingly, they 'undertake to work with renewed determination to enforce', among other things, the rule of law; the equality of all citizens before the law; individual and collective freedoms; the right to participate in free, credible and democratic political processes; and adherence to the separation of powers, including protection for the independence of the judiciary and the effectiveness of parliaments.

The Declaration on Democracy, Political, Economic and Corporate Governance also committed participating states to establish an African Peer Review Mechanism (APRM) to promote adherence to and fulfilment of its commitments. The Durban summit adopted a document setting out the stages of peer review and the principles by which the APRM should operate; further core documents were adopted at a meeting in Abuja in March, 2003, including a Memorandum of Understanding to be signed by governments wishing to undertake the peer review.

The policies of the New Partnership for Africa's Development appear to be emancipating and empowering. However, the implementation of those policies remains in the meantime, a myth. This is largely because since the funding of the partnership is based on the voluntary contributions of member states of the Union, most of them are not willing or eager to contribute. Therefore, if the activities of the partnership are to be felt by Africans, it should be made mandatory for all the member states of the African Union to contribute to its activities. Failure to do so will render it a toothless bulldog.

Partners
- UN Economic Commission for Africa (UNECA)
- African Development Bank
- Development Bank of Southern Africa (DBSA)
- Investment Climate Facility (ICF)
- African Capacity Building Foundation
- Office of the UN Under-Secretary-General and Special Adviser on Africa
- IDC (The Industrial Development Corporation) - Sponsor of NEPAD

Programme

The eight priority areas of NEPAD are: political, economic and corporate governance; agriculture; infrastructure; education; health; science and technology; market access and tourism; and environment.

During the first few years of its existence, the main task of the NEPAD Secretariat and key supporters was the popularisation of NEPAD's key principles, as well as the development of action plans for each of the sectoral priorities. NEPAD also worked to develop partnerships with international development finance institutions—including the World Bank, G8, European Commission, UNECA and others—and with the private sector.[7]

After this initial phase, more concrete programmes were developed, including:
- The Comprehensive Africa Agriculture Development Programme (CAADP), aimed at assisting the launching of a 'green revolution' in Africa, based on a belief in the key role of agriculture in development.
- The Programme for Infrastructure Development in Africa (PIDA) which comprises numerous trans-boundary infrastructure projects in the four sectors transport, energy,

water and ICT, aimed at boosting intra-African trade and interconnecting the continent.

- The NEPAD Science and Technology programme, including an emphasis on research in areas such as water science and energy.

- The "e-schools programme", adopted by the HSGIC in 2003 as an initiative to equip all 600,000 primary and secondary schools in Africa with IT equipment and internet access within 10 years, in partnership with several large IT companies. See NEPAD E-School program

- The launch of a Pan African Infrastructure Development Fund (PAIDF) by the Public Investment Corporation of South Africa, to finance high priority cross-border infrastructure projects.

- Capacity building for continental institutions, working with the African Capacity Building Foundation, the Southern Africa Trust, UNECA, the African Development Bank, and other development partners. One of NEPAD's priorities has been to strengthen the capacity of and linkages among the Regional Economic Communities.

- NEPAD was involved with the Timbuktu Manuscripts Project although it is not entirely clear to what extent.

Economic, Social and Cultural Council

- The Economic, Social and Cultural Council (ECOSOCC) is an advisory organ designed to give civil society organisations (CSOs) a voice within the African Union institutions and decision-making processes. It is provided for under Article 22 of the Union's Constitutive Act, but does not have its own protocol, relying rather on statutes created or approved by the Assembly of the Union that have a lesser legal status and can more easily be amended.

[171]Economic, Social and Cultural Council is made up of civil society organisations from a wide range of sectors including labour, business and professional groups, service providers and policy think tanks both from within Africa and African Diaspora.[172] It was formally established in 2005 and it seeks to build partnership between African governments and civil society.

• The 150-member General Assembly was launched in September, 2008 replacing the Council's initial interim structure; and it is made up of 144 elected representatives, two from each member state, 10 operating at level, eight at continental level and 20 from diasporas, and six representatives of civil society organisations nominated by the African Union Commission (Authority), to be the highest decision-making body of the organ. Apart from that, there is a 15-member standing committee with representatives from the five regions of Africa to coordinate the work of the organ; 10 sectoral cluster committees for feeding opinion and inputs into the policies and programmes of the African Union. The council is also composed of a five-person credentials committee for determining the eligibility of civil society organisations representatives to contest election or participate in the processes of the organs. [173]

• The statutes of the Economic, Social and Cultural Council have set the criteria for membership of the council which include that candidates must be national, regional, continent or African Diaspora; civil organisations, restriction to undertake regional or internal activities; they

171   Chitiga R. op. cit. p.33
172   Chitiga R. op. cit. p.27. See also Article 22(2) of the Union's Constitutive Act
173   Ibid

should have objectives and principles that are consistent with the principles and objectives of African Union and/ or meet the general conditions of eligibility for the granting of observer status to non-governmental organisations. In addition to that the candidates must show proof that the ownership and management of the civil society organisation is made up of not less than 50 percent of Africans or African Diaspora; and they must show that the resources of the organisation derives at least 50 percent from contributions of the members of the organisation.[174]

• The interim structures of the Economic, Social and Cultural Council were established in 2005, under the leadership of the Interim chairperson, Wangari Maathai of Kenya. Elections to the Council structures were finally held in 23 member states and at continental level in 2007. The eight members of the Economic, Social and Cultural Council's Assembly at the continental level are the pan-African Lawyers Union (PALU), the Organisation of African Trade Union (OATU), the Pan-African Employers Federation (PAEF), the African International Development Programme Voice, the Network of African Peace Builders, and women groups such as the Pan-African Women Organisation (PAWO) and Femmes African Solidarities (FAS).[175] Although elections had not been completed, the official launch of the Council's General Assembly took place in Dares Salaam, Tanzania, on 9th September, 2008, the Council's Assembly held a meeting in Abuja, Nigeria, to discuss a strategic plan for the organ

---

174 Ibid
175 Ibid

and began a review of the Economic, Social and Cultural Council's statutes. [176]

• As strategic and all-embracing as this organ appears to be, it remains a rubber stamp of the Assembly of the Union thereby rendering it ineffective and valueless to the African citizens. Even if the civil society organisations decide to make an input in the affairs of the Union to the Council, such an impute will be dumped by the Assembly of the Union, in case it does not favour the "Strongmen of the Union." To this end, it is submitted that the Council should be given direct functions to perform for and on behalf of the Union without being subject to the Assembly of the Union. This is the only way civil society organisations can participate in the affairs of the Union, and consequently the ordinary citizens will benefit there from.

---

176 Hanson S. "The African Union: Update 2009" A document of Open Society Initiative of Southern Africa, retrieved from www.africa.union.org/root/AU/AUC/Departments/BCP/CIDO/cido.htm downloaded on 7/7/2010

CHAPTER FIVE

The Legal Effects of the Activities of African Union

Introduction

The preceding chapter, that is to say, chapter four, dealt greatly or extensively with the African Union's economic framework and the functions thereof. Those functions have impacts on member states in one way or the other, be they negative or positive. An appraisal of those impacts to be undertaken herein will reveal the Union's speedometer of performance, the strength and weaknesses, for a better Africa. Since the Union was created to tackle the challenges facing the continent in the new millennium, its performance is highly expected to have had positive impacts on the citizenry. Though some analysts would "justifiably" argue that it is too early to judge its performance, however, a voyage into the terrain of the Union's performance will justify the schools of thought. The assessment herein is streamlined to areas of constitutional government, restoration of peace in member states and protection of human rights.

Intervention in Support of Constitutional Government

In the spirit of promoting democratic principles and institutions, popular participation and good governance as contained in Article 3(g) of the Constitutive Act of the African Union, the African Charter on Democracy, Elections and Governance was adopted at the 8th ordinary session of the African Union Assembly in Addis Ababa, Ethiopia, in 2007. Some scholars contend that, in a historical sense, the charter on Democracy,

Elections and Governance draws reference from the 1981 African Charter on Human and Peoples Rights.[177] The charter which is the fulcrum of the discussion under this subheading has a positive and negative element which calls for consideration. This document keeps focus and attention on democratisation, a process that by definition is universally long-term in nature throughout the world since Africa plays very important role in the global democracy. The charter contains provisions that urge member states to take wide measures to promote democracy in their territories by enforcing the provisions and respecting them in their spirit and fact. However, the discussion herein will focus primarily on Articles 17-26 for they constitute the core of the charter in that they deal specifically with elections, threat to democracy and constitutional order as well as what can be done to deter or reverse such actions. Article 17 provides that state parties should "establish and strengthen independent and impartial election bodies." This provision has been criticised by some analysts as they contend that "there is a potential contradiction in the notion that a government has the responsibility to 'establish' an independent electoral body."[178] It has been argued further that it is important to emphasise the autonomous and self-managing nature of these bodies, and that it would be helpful for such bodies to be permanent, rather than ad-hoc in character.[179] This argument, with respect, is narrowly based as the scholars fail to recognise and realise that some member states like Nigeria have made the electoral bodies embedded in their constitutions thereby making them permanent. Nevertheless, as

---

177 Mcmahon E.R. "The African Charter on Democracy, Elections and Governance: a Positive Step on a Long Path" (2007), p.1 a document of African Governance Monitoring and Advocacy Project.

178 Mcmahon E.R. and Baker S. Piecing a Democratic Quilt: Universal Norm and Regional Organisation (Bloomfield: Kumerian press, 2006) p.26

179 Ibid

rightly argued, the management of those bodies and autonomy are what remain heady issues. Most of the so-called "independent bodies" are stage-managed by the executive and the legislative arms of government in order to achieve their aims. Articles 18 and 19 deal with the advisor and missions which will be sent to member states in consultation with the African Union Commission while Article 20 emphasises the importance of pre-election observation missions, a key point given that the conditions under legitimacy of election is determined, do not relate simply to the immediate period around election day. They are often set in advance of this period, and continue through the dispute resolution process subsequent to elections.[180] The duration as to how long the missions should be in a particular country is said to be silent. It is therefore, possible that such missions may be superficial in nature without any visible impact. Article 22 of the charter raises concern because it commits state parties to creating a "conducive environment" to "independent and impartial" domestic non-Governmental Organisation monitoring, which in and of itself is positive.[181] This presumably leaves it to the member states government, however, to determine the independence and impartiality of the monitoring effort. If, in the view of the host government, this is seen as lacking the charter's wording since it permits the government to forbid the functioning of host country non-Governmental organisation observation monitoring efforts. Such a decision could potentially be based solely on a government's own subjective, and potentially biased, interpretation of the non-Governmental organisation's impartiality. It has been argued that in order to ensure uniformity and adherence to commonly accepted criteria; it would be useful to

---

180 BJornlund E.C. Beyond Free and Fair, Monitoring Elections and Building Democracy (Washington DC: Wilson Centre Press, 2004) p.204
181 Mcmahon E.R. op. cit. p.2

emphasise the existing internationally accepted norms regarding the functioning of domestic non-Governmental organisation monitoring efforts.[182] If standard or criteria of choosing such monitoring non-Governmental organisation is left in the hands of the host country, it would rather be biased as government of such a country will be looking for the organisations that will give favouring reports. It is submitted that in order to ensure fairness and justice, the commission of the Union should examine the monitoring non-Governmental organisations with a view to accrediting them for the assignment.

Article 23 of the charter is critically and fundamentally important in that it specifies that illegal means of accessing or maintaining power constitute an unconstitutional change of government. This Article is clearly based on African experiences and realities particularly in relation to unconstitutional change of government by military authorities in some countries. The fear or reality of mercenaries overthrowing governments has a long track of record in some African countries such as Congo, Sao Tome, Comoros, Benin Republic and Guinea Bissau even in the wake of institutionalised democracy in Africa. Similarly, there is a long elections lacking legitimacy being accepted by the African Union, notwithstanding the 2000 declaration on unconstitutional change of government, and advocacy efforts by non-Governmental organisations and other factors.[183] For the purpose of clarity, Article 23 defines "illegal means" of changing government to include (a) military coup; (b) intervention by mercenaries to replace a democratically elected government;

---

182 The recent and relevant documents in this regard are: the 2005 "Declaration of Principles for International Elections Observers", "Code of Conduct for International Election Observation" issued by United Nations etc.

183 See the situations in Kenya in 2007 and Zimbabwe where Robert Mugabe stuck to power in spite of wide victory by opposition.

(c) the replacement of a democratically elected government by armed rebels and dissidents; and (d) the refusal of an incumbent to surrender power after a free, fair and regular election. The amended protocol to the charter under Article 23 also includes an additional definition of unconstitutional change of government that any amendment or revision of the constitution or legal instruments, which is an infringement on the principles of democratic change.

Some commentators might argue that by broadening this provision, it has in effect been watered down (as the main Article 23 had clearly targeted attempts to lift term limitations). However, it can be authoritatively argued or interpreted that it is a step ahead as it would appear to cover possible scenarios of what came to be known as democratic backsliding.[184] While not as blatant as military coups, this refers to actions which have the effect of chipping away at democratic freedoms, with cumulative effect of maintaining government power illegitimately. These can include among others limitations on freedom of speech, provisions designed to sideline potential or real opposition candidates and/or parties, or limitation on legislature to act as a meaningful check or balance on the executive arm of government. They also include situations which a democratically elected government engages in all forms of anti-democratic actions. The provision of Article 23 and amendment thereto reflects the true situation in Africa. This is exemplified in the recent scenario in Cote d'Ivoire wherein the defeated incumbent President Laurent Gbagbo hurriedly amended the country's constitution by introducing and constituting a "Constitutional council" as having final say in election matters. This certainly

---

184 This concept is closely related to the "illiberal democracy" phenomenon first articulated by Fareed Zakaria in "The Rise of Illiberal Democracy" published in November/December 1997 issue of Foreign Affairs, p.3

is not the constitutional change as provided in the Article 23 of the African Charter on Democracy, Elections and Governance.

What then can be said to be the impact of the African Union on the member states in relation to constitutional government? Can the Union's role in this regard be said to have had positive effect on member states? The questions can best be answered in a cold voice.

The legal framework for constitutional government has been put in place by the Union ranging from the Constitutive Act to other charters as well as protocols. These instruments, however, cannot work without the sincere and genuine commitment of the African leaders. The plausible provisions of the said legal instrument remain mere expressions on the paper without practicality of the contents therein. The recent happening on the African continent is a clear indication that the African Union is not a solution to the numerous socio-political challenges facing the continent. The protest in Egypt which led to the resignation of the former President, Hosni Mubarak, was the manifestation of the weakness or frailty of the African Union which is said to be the voice of Africa. In situations like this, under normal circumstances, the Union should have taken steps to enforce the wishes of the masses. May be, Egyptians and other Africans in countries like Tunisia refused to refer their matters to the Union because similar cases were reported to the Union in countries like Kenya and Zimbabwe but to the greatest chagrin of the Civil Society Groups in those countries, there was no positive response from the Union. The "revolution" that took place in the Arab countries of North Africa is an eye opened to other African countries which hitherto relied on the African Union as a solution to socio-political problems in their respective countries.

Article 25 of the African Charter on Democracy, Elections and Governance seems to have suggested a solution to the perennial problem of the "unconstitutional change of government", however, a careful consideration of the article reveals that it is weak in itself. Though the article prescribes punishment for unconstitutional change of government as contained in Article 23 of the Charter, it fails to specify the nature of sanctions to be imposed on such erring member states, thereby leaving the issue of sanctions as vague as contained in the Union's Constitutive Act. The Article only empowers the Peace and Security Council to impose the sanctions of suspending the erring member state from the Union activities. If the provisions of Article 25 were anything to go by, the situation in Cote d'Ivoire would have taken a different dimension. The Union would have taken a definite stand on the issue instead of considering "other options". Although the African Charter on Democracy, Elections and Governance derive its inspiration from the Inter-American Democratic Charter, the implementation of both charters makes them to be strange bedfellows.[185] It was the President of Mali, Alpha Omar Konane, the then Chairman of the Organisation of African Unity who attended "Emerging Democracy Forum" in Yemen in June 1999 that learned about the Organisation of Inter-American States suspension of governments which came to power through undemocratic means. After he asked his Embassy in Washington DC to procure the Inter-American Charter, he then handed over the idea to the former organisation which bequeathed it to the African Union.[186]

Additionally, as evidenced in the structure of the African Peer Review Mechanism and its function vis-à-vis the actual cases such as Kenya, Zimbabwe and currently, Cote d'Ivoire, the overall African Union's approach towards democracy promotion appears to be more oriented towards carrot rather than

---

185   Mcmahon "piercing Democratic Quilt..." p.134
186   Ibid

stick. Some commentators have argued that this demonstrate a fundamental lack of political will to address the challenges to democratic development head on.[187] It has also been contended in the alternative that another interpretation would emphasize the legitimacy of a more gradualist approach based on African traditions of consensus and compromise rather than more "western" notions of rapid progress based on conflict and a merely zero-sum winner-loser exercise of democracy.[188] The problem with the latter approach of course, is that it can take a long time before it becomes clear whether this is a legitimate approach or simply a window dressing developed by governments that have little vested interest in promoting meaningful and credible democratisation processes. This is an issue that has played out within the African Union over the short to medium term of its existence.

It must be stated that the African Charter on Democracy, Elections and Governance is in and of itself a move in the positive direction; the proof of the pudding always remains in the eating, its implementation. In this way, it is submitted that it should currently not be seen as a panacea but rather as an encouraging or positive step in the right direction. Until there will be reawakening by the African leaders to the socio-political challenges facing the continent, there will be no rapid development in Africa. The African notions of "consensus and compromise" must be jettisoned in the interest of the citizenry.

Restoration of Peace in Conflict Member-States
For there to be meaningful development in any society, peace must reign supreme otherwise the reverse will be the case. In recognition of that fact, the drafters of the African Un-

---

187 Ibid, p.136
188 Ibid

ion's Constitutive Act did think wise to make peace part of the Act. The Constitutive Act provides that the Union may intervene in restoring peace therein.[189] In furtherance to the Union's commitment to restoring peace in member states, in May, 2004 the African Union officially launched its new Peace and Security Council. At the launch, African leaders emphasized that the Peace and Security Council's potential significance claiming that its establishment "marks historic watershed in Africa's progress towards resolving its conflicts and building of a durable peace and security order".[190] In re-commitment to the issue of peace and security in the continent, African leaders at the special session on the Consideration and Resolution of Conflicts in Africa held in Tripoli on 31st August, 2009 collectively made the pledge as follows:

> ...We are determined to deal once and for all with the scourge of conflicts and violence on our continent, acknowledging our shortcomings and errors, committing our resources and our best people, and missing no opportunity to push forward the agenda of conflict prevention, peace-keeping, peacemaking and post conflict reconstruction. We, as leaders, simply cannot bequeath the burden of conflicts to the next generation of Africans. [191]

Before the launch of the Peace and Security Council of the African Union in 2004, there was already in existence a

---

189   See Article 4(i) and (j)

190   Statement of Commitment to Peace and Security in Africa, issued by the Heads of State and Government of the member states of the Peace and Security Council of the African Union (AU documents, PSC/AHG/St (x, 25 May 2004) p.1

191   See the message of Mr. Jean Ping, Chairperson of the Commission of the African Union on International Day of Peace, 21st September 2010 retrieved from www.makepeacehappen, on 31st December, 2010

mechanism for conflict prevention, management and resolution of Organisation of African Unity, which was adopted at the 29th ordinary session of the Organisation's Assembly held in Cairo, Egypt in 1993.[192] The mechanism's primary objective initially was the anticipation and prevention of conflicts. This focus on prevention emerged after a series of debates in Dakar in 1992 and Addis Ababa in 1993 wherein the organisation's members took a consensus decision not to involve the organization in peace keeping operations. Optimistically, it was hoped that a focus on preventive diplomacy would dramatically reduce the need for subsequent peace operations on the continent. The consensus however, proved to be short-lived. The mass killings in Burundi and Rwanda in 1993-1994 in particular, caused the Organisation to revisit its self-imposed ban on peacekeeping operations on the continent. This began with a series of internal debates organised by Organisation of African Unity Secretariat and the circulation of the background paper summarising the issues. These discussions in turn, led to the Organisation's 1995 summit in Addis Ababa endorsing the idea that ready contingents should be earmarked within African armies for deployment in peacekeeping operations. Despite this change in principle, throughout the 1990s, the Organisation continued to define its priority as conflict prevention arguing that the primary responsibility for peacekeeping in Africa lay with the United Nations.

The problem with this position became increasingly evident as the United Nations proved reluctant to take the lead resolving African conflicts. In Liberia, Sierra Leone and Guin-

---

192   Williams P.D. "Peace and Security Council of African Union: Evaluating an Embryonic International Institution" being a paper presented to the panel "Do International Institutions have a future in International Security?" at School of International Affairs, Washington University, USA on 26-30 March, 2008, p.3

ea-Bissau, groups of West African States used Economic Community of West African States as a vehicle to respond to these conflicts.[193] This led to the view by some member states that the Organisation of African Unity was a defunct and anachronistic institution therefore, it should be closed down. This soon gained upper hand within the Organisation, culminating in the decision taken at the 37th ordinary session of Assembly in Lusaka in July, 2001 to review the structures and working methods of the Organisation's mechanism in the light of the establishment of a new African Union.[194] The next practical step was taken when the Organization of African Unity's Secretary-General produced a document titled "Background Documentation on Review Structures, Procedures and Working Methods of the Central Organ".[195] This document served as the conceptual starting point for the drafting of the Peace and Security Council Protocol. After mooting a range of alternative names, including Peace Council, African Security Council and Council for Security, it was unanimously agreed at the second brainstorming retreat in South Africa in March 2002 that the new organ should be referred to as Peace and Security Council. The outcome of this was the adoption of the protocol relating to the establishment of Peace and Security Council of the African Union in Durban on 9th July, 2002. The protocol came into force in March 2003 and the Council officially began its work in 2004.

Pursuant to Article 5(2) of the African Union Constitutive Act, Article 2(1) of the Protocol establishing the Peace and Security Council as a "standing decision-making organ for the prevention, management and resolution of conflict" that should be

---

193 Ibid
194 Cilliers J. and Sturman K. "Challenge Facing African Union's Peace and Security Council" in African Security Review (2004) p.97
195 Ibid p.114

a collective security and early-warning arrangement to facilitate timely and efficient response to conflict and crisis situations in Africa.

On question of whether the Peace and Security Council has carried out its functions and missions competently and efficiently, there are divergent positions by different schools of thought. Some commentators have argued that considering the few years of the Council's existence, it has performed more positively than negatively.[196] In buttressing the argument, it has been contended that even under severely strenuous conditions, individual African Union Peacekeepers have performed admirably.[197] According to this school of thought, the Council's record on implementing its sanctions regimes has been much more positive. For instance on 4th August, 2005, Mauritania was suspended from the Union because of the coup de tat that had taken place there. In this case, no sooner had the Peace and Security Council adopted this position, the African Union's Deputy Legal Counsel went into the Assembly Summit Meeting and told the delegation from Mauritania to leave the chamber immediately. Again, that time, a similar situation occurred in Togo and its representatives were still quickly instructed to leave the Peace and Security Council's chamber in conformity with the decision. This position with respect, does not reflect the true state of things.

As rightly argued, the Peace and Security Council has devoted relatively little attention to the prevention of conflict and addressing structural issues that encourage "bad governance".[198] Ultimately, the Council needs to decide whether it wants to fo-

---

196 Williams P.D. op. cit. p.15
197 Williams G.O. and Cssis V. Protecting Two Million Internally Displaced: The Success and Shorting of the African Union in Darfur (London: Brooking Institutions Press, 2005) p.34
198 Williams P.D. op. cit. p.5

cus on a more efficient fire service or building better fire-proof houses. To date, the Council has clearly opted to act as a fire extinguisher, dealing with issues after they erupt forgetting its role of preventing conflicts. It seems that in order for a country to make it onto the Council's agenda, it needs to witness the emergence of an open rebellion or serious insurgency. For instance, despite the suffering caused by Robert Mugabe's regime and the purported re-election victory, no attempt was made to put Zimbabwe on the Council's agenda as Council's response to the violent aftermath of Kenya's elections in December 2007 remains fresh in our memories.

The Peace and Security Council's response to the role Ethiopia played in the crisis in Somalia is another concern. This started when Ethiopian forces in Somalia and those forces loyal to the Somali Transitional Federal Government forcibly ejected the Union of Islamic Courts from Mogadishu, killing many of its fighters in the process.[199] Ethiopia's official justifications fluctuated between self-defence and assisting the Transitional Federal Government assume its rightful status.[200] In either way, Ethiopia's military operations were undertaken without the mandate of the Peace and Security Council. Ethiopia was not sanctioned by the Council, probably because at that time, Addis Ababa was the seat of the Council as well as its member. The first sign that Ethiopia's seat on the Council might cause problems came when Commissioner Konare initially contacted representatives of Arab League apparently because of Addis Ababa's presence on the Council. Given that Ethiopia was a party to the conflict in Somalia, its representative should have withdrawn from the deliberations of the Council after briefing session as provided

---

199 Ibid p.15
200 Vihdego W.Z. "Ethiopia's Military Action Against the Union of Islamic Courts and Others in Somalia" an International Comparative Law Quarterly (2007) pp.666-667

under Article 8(9) of the Peace and Security Council's Protocol. The Article provides that:

> *Any member of Peace and Security Council which is party to a conflict under consideration by the Peace and Security Council shall not participate in either the discussion or the decision making process relating to that conflict or situation. Such member shall be invited to present its case to the Peace and Security Council as appropriate, and shall, thereafter, withdraw from proceedings.*

However, as it turned out, the Ethiopian representative not only remained in the meeting but sought to chair it, arguing that her country was not a party to the conflict.[201] After an hour of argument, it was decided that the representative from Gabon would chair the final part of the meeting but Ethiopian representative continued to participate in the deliberation. It is submitted that the continued stay of Ethiopian representative in the session violated the rule of natural justice which states that nobody can be a judge in his own case.

Analysts have argued that the compromise by the Peace and Security Council in the case involving Ethiopia was not the first case.[202] Similar examples are prevalent in relation to the conflict in Darfur. In this case, Sudan was an initial member of the Peace and Security Council. During this period, it was responsible for obstructing the Council's deliberations on a number of occasions. For instance, in late 2005, the Commission of the Union, wanted a meeting of Peace and Security Council on Darfur to discuss video evidence it had received that the Government of Sudan was painting its war planes in the African Union

---

201 Williams P.D. op. cit.
202 Ibid, p.16

colours and then using them in campaigns against Darfur rebels and civilians. While Sudan held the Council's chair, it was impossible to hold this kind of deliberation, had to be postponed. The recent political crisis in Cote d'Ivoire has clearly shown the weakness and ill-performance of the Peace and Security Council. The response or reaction of the Council to the crisis does not augur well for the peace of African continent. No wonder, the Arab countries of North Africa have resorted to "self-help" in form of protest to express their dissatisfaction with the "long period regimes of dictatorship" in their territories. Though some observers have attributed the poor performance of the Peace and Security Council to the poor funding from member states,[203] it is submitted that whichever way the argument will go, the Union, through its Peace and Security Council, has failed to bring the positive and/or needed impact on the continent. In countries where crisis occurred but there is relative calm such as Liberia, Sierra Leone, Comoros, Democratic Republic of Congo and Sudan, the "Peace and Security Council may well provide political support and legitimacy to operations but will inevitably play a secondary role to the United Nations."[204] This shows that but for the role of the United Nations, missions in the crisis stricken countries in Africa, the continent would not have experienced the relative calm currently prevailing therein.

It is submitted that for the African Union, and Peace and Security Council in particular, to have positive impact on the continent, whatever is needed for its full performance, be it adequate funding, staffing as well as secretariat, efforts should be intensified by all the stakeholders to ensure that the aims of its creation are achieved. It is the Union's inability to control crisis in the region that resulted in the referendum on the cessation

---

203 Ibid, p.17
204 Ibid

of Southern Sudan from the North. This is not a good record for the Union.

Protection and Promotion of Human and People's Rights

The concept of human rights is as old as man himself, the existence of man is dependent on his fundamental rights. In realizing this fact, man through his ingenuity fashioned ways of protecting those rights in order to harness them for peaceful co-existence in the society. The concern for the promotion and protection or universal respect for, and observance of, human rights and fundamental freedoms may be traced to humanist traditions of the Renaissance, to the struggle for self-determination, independence and equality that has taken place and is still proceeding in many parts of the world; to the philosophical concepts developed by such men like John Locke of England, Jean Jacques Rousseau of France, Thomas Jefferson of United States of America, Karl Marx of Germany and V.I. Lenin of Russia. The campaign by these philosophers resulted in the events such as the issuance of the Magnacarta by King John of England in 1215, the adoption of the Declaration of Independence by representatives of the 13 North Colonies in 1776, the adoption of the Declaration of Rights of man and of the citizens by the National Assembly of France in 1798, and the publication of the Communist Manifesto in 1848. [205]

At the first half of the 20th Century, at the close of the First World War, international concern with human rights found expression in certain provisions of the covenant of the League of Nations. State members of the League accepted the obligation to endeavour to secure and maintain fair and humane conditions of labour for men, women and children, as well as to ensure

---

205   Olakanmi O.A. Handbook on Human Rights (Nigeria: Panaf Press, 2007) p.1

the just treatment of the indigenous inhabitants of their colonies. The collapse of the League of Nations paved way for the emergence of the United Nations and its purposes include inter alia achievement of international co-operation in promoting and encouraging respect for human rights and for fundamental freedom for all without distinction as to race, sex, language or religion.[206] Apart from the human rights provisions contained in the United Nations' charter, the United Nations also adopted other instruments such as International Covenant on Economic, Social and Cultural Rights; the International Covenant on Civil and Political Rights as well as the optional protocol to the International Covenant on Civil and Political Rights. The adoption of Universal Declaration of Human Rights in 1948 was to serve as a common standard of achievement for all peoples and nations, to the end that every individual and every organ of society, keeping the declaration constantly in mind by teaching and educating to promote respect for the rights and by progressive measures, national and international, to ensure their effective and universal recognition and observance.[207]

In answer to the global call for the promotion and protection of human rights, the Organisation of African Unity in its charter stipulated the objectives to include among others, that "freedom, equality, justice and dignity" were essential objectives for the achievement of the legitimate aspirations of the African peoples. It was in line with those objectives that the organization in 1981 at Nairobi, Kenya, adopted African charter on Human Rights and Peoples' Rights with a view to advancing the course of human rights in Africa. In order to achieve the provisions of the charter, the African Commission on Human and Peoples' Rights was established in 1986.

---

206 Ibid
207 Ibid, p.5

In 1998, a protocol to the African charter on Human and Peoples' Rights to establish an African Court on Human and Peoples' Rights was adopted.

Upon the transition from Organisation of African Unity to African Union, most of the structures of the former were inherited by the latter including the court. The protocol for the establishment of the court came into force in 2004.[208] The pertinent question that remains unattended to is despite the adoption of various laws or charters respecting human and peoples' rights, what has been the level of compliance by member states of the African Union to the laws? By the provisions of Article 1 of African charter on Human and Peoples Rights the "member states of the Organisation of African Unity parties to the charter shall recognise the rights, duties and freedoms enshrined in the charter and shall undertake to adopt legislative measures to give to them". This imposes an obligation on the state parties to enforce the obligations or rights therein. In LAWYERS FOR HUMAN RIGHTS v. SWAZILAND[209] the complainant argued that by ratifying the African charter and not adopting legislative and other measures to bring 1973 proclamation in conformity with the charter, the respondent state had violated Article 1 of African charter on Human and Peoples' Rights. The commission in its ruling concluded that the use of the term other measures in Article 1 provides state parties with a wide choice of measures to use to deal with human rights problems. That in the present situation when a decree has been passed by the Head of State abrogating the constitution, it was incumbent on the same Head of State and other relevant institutions in the country to demonstrate good faith and either reinstate the constitution or amend

---

208   See "AU Treaties and their Status" retrieved from www.african-union.org/root/AU/documents/Treaties/treaties.htm, on 22nd January, 2011
209   Communications 251/2002

the decree to bring it in conformity with the charter provisions during or after ratifications.

Similarly, in CIVIL LIBERTY ORGANISATION (CLO) v. NIGERIA,[210] the complainant petitioned that the Political Parties Dissolution Decree 1994 under the Abacha government which revoked the Act incorporating the African charter into Nigerian law was illegal. The commission declared that given that Nigeria ratified the African charter in 1983, it is presently a convention in force in Nigeria. If Nigeria wished to withdraw its ratification, it would have to undertake international process involving notice, which it had not done. "Nigeria cannot negate the effect of its ratification of the charter through domestic action. Nigeria remains under the obligation to guarantee the rights of its citizens." Again, in the case of COMMISSION NATIONALE DES DROIT DE L'HOMME EST DES LIBERTES v. CHAD[211] the commission held that in the context of the on-going civil war in that territory the charter specified in Article 1 that the state parties shall not only recognise the rights, duties and freedoms adopted by the charter, but they should also undertake measures to give effect to them. The commission held that the African charter, unlike other human rights instruments, does not allow for state parties to derogate from their treaty obligations during emergency situations. Thus, even a civil war in Chad cannot be used as an excuse by the state to violate or permit the violation of rights in the African charter.

The above authorities have created an insight into the human rights situation in Africa. The promotion and protection of human and peoples' rights in Africa, though beautifully provided for in legal instruments, remains the most vexed issue. African leaders remain adamant to the full implementation of

---

210 No. 129/94
211 Commission No. 74/92

the charter and other protocols related thereto. The recent happenings in some of the African countries clearly indicate that the human and peoples' rights have been relegated to the background without an eyebrow. Since the creation of African Union, the much touted promotion and protection of human and peoples' rights have become subject to academic debate. Some observers and analysts have contended that the refusal of the African Union to prosecute Hissene Habre, former President of Chad, for crimes against humanity was the bane of the crusade against human rights violation in Africa.[212] It has been contended further that "with determination, the African Union could have used the case of Habre as a test to adopt a far more proactive stance to show to the world at large that something could change."[213] Failure of the Union to take a decisive stance on the issue gave room for other African countries to follow suit. For instance, the action of the self-acclaimed winner of presidential election in Cote d'Ivoire, Laurent Gbagbo without resistance from the Union has shown that the fight against human rights abuses in Cote d'Ivoire, Laurent Gbagbo without resistance from the Union has shown that the fight against human rights abuses in the continent has been kept in the coffins. Gbagbo and his cohorts have destroyed precious innocent lives in Cote d'Ivoire through the use of army loyal to him.

Again, the happenings in Libya under Muammar Gadhafi are the last straw that broke the camel's back. Following the mass protest against the leadership of the Arab World, the tsunami found its way into Libya. However, instead of toeing the line of honour like other leaders of Tunisia and Egypt in Africa, "the strong man of Africa" decided to use force against

---

212 Baker B. "Twilight of Impunity for Africa's Presidential Criminals" 25 Third World Q. (2004) pp.1487-1499
213 Ibid

the innocent and defenceless citizens of the country. This has resulted in massive killings of the citizens who have the right to decide who would be their leader. Even in the face of this, African Union remains undecided as to the appropriate measures to be taken against Gadhafi or Libya. Instead, it is the United Nations which is the world watchdog that has decided to declare "no-fly-zone" in the country wherein the world forces are trying to neutralise Gadhafi's forces. Despite that, Gadhafi has vowed to continue with the fight. These practical examples have clearly shown that the legal instruments put in place for the promotion and protection of human and peoples' rights are toothless bull dog. It is submitted that unless and until the African Union's approach to human rights is changed to the right direction, the so-called fight against human rights abuses and crimes against humanity in Africa will remain a myth rather than reality.

CHAPTER SIX

Social Effects of the Activities of African Union

Introduction

Apart from the legal effects of the Union's performance discussed in one of the chapters above, there are social effects which the Union in its almost ten years of existence and performance has had on the African citizenry. In this chapter, the social effects such as the health of the Africans as pledged by member states to tackle the problems therein and the commitment thereto as well as the economic co-operation and member states are extensively considered.

Fight against Health Threatening (Diseases) Issues

Health, it is usually said, is wealth; but it goes beyond that. It will be apt to say that health is life because life without good health is meaningless. It is in the light of the above that the World Health Organisation Assembly made the "Declaration of Health for All" in 1977; and later in 1978 in Alma-Ata adopted the primary health care approach as the strategy by which the ultimate objective of the "Health for All" would be attained. As part of the global movement, African countries developed health-for-all strategies and incorporated them within their national health development plans with a view to addressing some urgent needs such as the development of human resources for health; promotion of environmental health; control of communicable diseases and strengthening of health systems.[214]

It has been contended that promotion of access to universal primary health services remains an important goal although the target of achieving this by 2000 was not attained.[215] Nevertheless, there have been some improvements in health care which should be intensified and would among others have to include investments in health especially child and maternal health, strengthening health systems and involving all actors, institutions and resources that undertake health actions with the primary intent of improving the health status of populations. Although the defining goal of a health system is to improve a population's health, other intrinsic goals include responsiveness to service users as determined by the way in which they are treated and ensuring that the financial burden of paying for health is fairly distributed across households.[216]

However, various constraints, it is argued, are being experienced in health delivery systems, namely weak health infrastructure, limited tools, inadequate human resource capacity, limited public financing to the health sector as a whole, and not only to disease-specific programme, poor management and planning as well as lack of integrated health systems and misapplication of human, technical and financial resources. Africa is said to have borne the heaviest burden of disease management due to communicable diseases especially HIV/AIDS, Ebola Virus Disease, Lassa fever, malaria and tuberculosis, as well as high child and maternal mortality, some of which are pre-

214   Gawanas B. "African Union and Health Challenges in Africa: Strategies and Initiatives on Health Care Delivery" p.1, a document of the African Union, retrieved from http://www.africa-union.org on 25th February, 2011
215   Ibid
216   Ibid

ventable. Non-communicable diseases such as mental illness and injuries are also said to be emerging as contributors to the disease burden; and this greatly impacts on the continent's resources. [217]

It is crystal clear that public health concerns remain with the emergence of HIV/AIDS. Malaria also remains one of the leading causes of illness and death in the continent; especially among children.[218] Childhood diseases attributed to respiratory infections, diarrhea disease, measles, malaria, polio and malnutrition account for a high rate of child mortality. Many of these are preventable if proper and accessible health care systems are in place. Pregnancy and childbirth have also resulted in the highest maternity mortality in the world leading to a situation where Africa accounts for the 20% of the world's birth, but contribute 40% of maternal deaths. Other related health issues include environmental concerns, behaviour and lifestyles, conflicts and migration which also expose people to the risk of disease and other epidemics as well as malnutrition.

In spite of the avowed commitment to sustainable health systems as contained in the Abuja Declaration which targets 15 percent of public spending for health by member states and the millennium development Goals (which are directly and indirectly related to health and development) the burden of disease has continued to increase. Again, the African Union Commission had developed a strategic plan (2005-2007) which placed emphasis on controlling the disease burden and promoting good health on the continent.[219] In this regard, the African Union places great importance on continental initiatives such as the

---

217 Ibid, p.2
218 Ibid
219 See African Union Commission Strategic Plan (2005-2007) on http://www.african-union. org retrieved on 21/1/2011

Bamako Initiative on Essential Medicines and the decade on traditional medicines. It has been argued that despite the efforts of the member states to invest in health and implement health strategies, the burden of disease or health crisis has continued to increase.[220] It is submitted that the above assertion is far from the truth. Analysts have rightly posited that having realised the abysmal performance in the area of health, the thirty-five Heads of State and Government, who attended the 15th ordinary summit of Africa Union in Kampala, Uganda pledged "to recommit themselves to an earlier declaration in Abuja in 2001, wherein they would devote 15 percent of their national budgets to health sector."[221] If the leaders could confess themselves of non-commitment to the earlier declaration in Abuja in 2001, then one wonders the nature of the "efforts by member states to invest in health and to implement health strategies" referred to by the author.

While Africa carries the highest burden of diseases and therefore needs to have health systems which can cope effectively with controlling the disease burden, the financial resources needed for that to happen has not been availably adequate. In realisation of this fact, and as stated above, the Heads of State and Government of the African Union committed themselves in the Abuja Declaration (2001) to allocate 15 percent of their national budget to health. However, assessment of the progress on this commitment reveals that four countries are currently allocating less than five percent, 25 countries allocate between five and ten percent and 13 countries between eleven and fourteen percent.[222] At present, only two countries are re-

---

220 Gawanas B. op. cit.
221 Hamza S. "How Committed are African Leaders to Child Maternal Health?" The Sunday Trust of August 8, 2010 p.28
222 Gawanas B. p.3

ported to have reached the 15 percent prescribed in the Abuja Declaration. Considering the high burden of diseases in Africa, the allocation of financial resources for health must be critically assessed with a view to increasing same.

Apart from inadequate financial resources allocated to the health sector by African leaders, there are other factors that inhibit the efficient functioning of health care system in Africa. One such inhibition is lack of cohesion in the sectoral policies. Many African countries allow disease specific programmes which do not look at the wider institutional contexts as agreed in the declarations adopted. In most cases, priority is placed on individual diseases like HIV infection or malaria but not on the strengthening of the entire health sector.[223] There needs to be an increased investment in the whole health sector that it can address adequately the complete range of causes of human illnesses. It is submitted that an effective health policy would address the health sector in a holistic and integrated manner rather than through fragmented disease approach. Specific interventions will find synergy with other sectoral issues such as infrastructural development, sanitation, nutrition, among others.

Another factor or challenge militating against effective health care delivery is human resource crisis in the sector. The crisis in the health sector workforce has become a major constraint to any development and improvement of the health status of most communities in Africa. This is said to have been attended to in various continental fora, ranging from health to migration, including the adoption of a Declaration on Human Resources for Health by the African Union policy organs.[224] New Partnership for Africa's Development (NEPAD), as the African

---

223 Ibid p.4
224 Ibid

Union development programme has also identified human resource development as one of its priorities. Nevertheless, most
African countries or governments do not pay attention to the
welfare of the health workers in their domain, thereby resulting
in incessant face-off or strikes. At present, in Nigeria, for instance, almost all the states of the federation are rocked in one
strike or the other by health workers. This usually results in the
unimaginable untimely deaths of those that would have con-
tributed to the growth of the country. There is no doubt that the
performance of the health systems in African countries depends
on human resources capacity. African governments often struggle with human resources capacity issues due to various factors such as misapplication of human resources as many health
professionals are employed in sectors other than the health sector.[225] Health professionals also leave their home country each
year to pursue better prospects in other countries both on and
off the continent or are driven out by low pay or poor working
conditions. This has resulted in poor quality of the labour force,
lack of technological advancement, limited productivity and
above all weakness of health systems, leading to a decline in the
quality of health care delivery. It is submitted that for there to
be quality health delivery in Africa, countries must ensure that
their health systems get the right number of service providers
with the right skills to the right place at the right time.

For a better health system, the African countries and
their leaders must uphold their "re-commitment" to health care
delivery as pledged at the African Union 15th ordinary summit in Kampala, Uganda. They must make sure that the 15%
budgetary allocation pledged to include in their national fiscal
expenditure is complied with. This will reduce the negative im-

---

225   For instance, a female medical doctor turned into a newscaster in Kiss F.M. Radio in
       Abuja due to desperation.

pacts the mal-functional health systems in the member states have on the citizenry. The African Union Commission should, through its science and technology research centre in Lagos, Nigeria, encourage alternative or traditional medicine, for there to be affordable health delivery system. This will help promote the right of African citizens to life, which is the most fundamental human right, and it is dependent on sound health.

Promotion of Economic Co-operation among Member States

In economic parlance, the concept of economic cooperation is also known as economic integration. In this context, both terms will be used interchangeably to refer to one concept and for the same purpose. It has been contended that the idea of integration is the one that is basically social. This is because the integration process is that one that realizes the cohesiveness of the society and it is essentially political in contents though the initial objectives would be purely economic. Whatever the form or aim of integration, there is always an element of political integration in the sense that the integrating states would of necessity have to surrender some aspects of their sovereignty with the aim of achieving the objectives of the integration. Some scholars have advanced reasons for economic integration to include: (a) economic integration or cooperation offers a viable strategy for accelerated economic development and infrastructural transformation; (b) it supports industrialisation process as projects otherwise beyond the competence of one member may be executed with the assistance and cooperation of other members; (c) it serves as a great stimulus to independence of actions on the part of developing countries by strengthening their negotiating capabilities; and (d) through the establishment and extension of payments and credit arrangements, trade could be facilitated and balance of payment problems gradually resolved.[226]

Historically, long before the establishment of Organisation of African Unity, African leaders had recognised that co-operation and integration among African countries in economic, social and cultural fields[227] are indispensable to the accelerated transformation and sustained development of African continent. This was concretized in 1963 in the objectives of the Organisation of African Unity[228] as contained in its charter as well as in the organisations summit in 1973 and 1976, and the Monrovia Declaration of 1979. In 1980, the Organisation of African Unity extra-ordinary summit adopted the Lagos plan of action, as a major step towards that goal. During that summit, African leaders stated their commitment individually as well as collectively to promote the economic integration of Africa in order to facilitate and reinforce social and economic intercourse. They also committed themselves to promote the economic and social development and integration of their economics, and to that end, to establish national, regional and sub-regional institutions leading to a dynamic and interdependent African economy, thus paving way for the eventual establishment of African Economic Community. [229]

• The commitments in the "Lagos Plan of Action" and "Final Act of Lagos" were translated into concrete form in Abuja, Nigeria, in June 1991 when the Organisation of African Unity Heads of State and Government signed

---

226 A Jomo M.A. and Adewale O. (eds) African Economic Community Treaty: Issues, Problems and Prospects (Lagos: NIALS Press, 1993) p.2
227 Ibid
228 This objective is reframed in the Constitutive Act of the African Union in Article 3(j)
229 Ajomo, ibid, p.3

the Treaty establishing the African Economic Community (hereinafter referred to as "The Community"). The Community Treaty has been in operation since May 1994 when the required number of instruments of ratification for its coming into force was deposited with the Secretary General of the Organisation of African Unity and the Community.

- At the "regional and sub-regional" levels, African countries have embarked on various programmes for the promotion of integration, and have established organisations and institutions to support their efforts.[230] So far, the African Economic Community has established direct working relations with the Economic Community of West African States (ECOWAS) in West Africa, the Economic Community of Central Africa and in the East and Southern Africa, the Common Market for East and Southern Africa (COMESA). In the Southern region, the Community has been dealing with the Southern African Development Community (SADC). In North Africa, there is the Arab Maghreb Union (ZAMU) which has no direct contact with the African Economic Community, so far. [231]

- Apart from Regional Economic Communities (RECs), there are other economic groupings like Economic and Monetary Union of West Africa and the Customs and Economic Union of Central Africa both of which are engaged in the promotion of integration. Though all these organizations were already in existence and operating before the African Economic Community Treaty was signed

---

230 See the document on African Economic Community, retrieved from http://www.un.org/afric/nepad.htm on 21/1/2011

231 See Articles 6 and 88 of the Abuja Treaty which deal with the activities of Regional Economic Communities

in Abuja in 1991. The Community and indeed African Union find them indispensable instruments in order to promote the socio-economic development of Africa and to face effectively the challenges posed by globalization. By the provision of Article 88 of the Abuja Treaty, the establishment of the African Economic Community is the final objective towards which the activities of Regional Economic Communities (existing and future ones) shall be geared. In recognition of this fact that Abuja Treaty has set up modalities for establishing African Economic Community, and they consist of six stages of variable duration over a transition period of not exceeding thirty four years, from the date of entry into force of the Treaty. Each of the stages consists of specific activities to be implemented concurrently.

- The first stage deals with strengthening of existing Regional Economic Communities and establishing new ones in regions where they do not exist; this takes five years. The second stage, which is an eight year programme deals with the establishment of tariff and non-tariff barriers, customs duties and internal taxes, and determination of time-table for the gradual liberalisation of regional and intra-community trade and for harmonisation of customs duties at regional levels. It also deals with strengthening of sectoral integrations, particularly in fields of trade, agriculture, money and finance, transport and communications industry and energy; and the coordination and harmonisation of Regional Economic Communities activities. The third stage considers the establishment of Free Trade Area customs union at regional level in a period of two years while the fourth stage (in two years) is concerned with coordination and harmonisation of tariff and non-tariff barriers among various Regional Economic Communities with a view to establishing a continental Customs Union. The fifth stage, which is a four year programme deals with establishment of an African Common Market which structures will be consolidated and strengthened at the sixth stage. This stage will also consider critically the free movement of people and factors of production; creation of single domestic market and Pan African Economic Monetary Union, African Central Bank and African Currency (within 5 years).

- The Abuja Treaty also provided for measures to be taken concurrently with regard to the formulation of multinational projects and programmes for the promotion of harmonious and balanced development among member states. However, the full implementation of the stages at the designated time remains an issue every serious minded African will ponder over it. As rightly argued (it may be wrong in others view) elsewhere in this work, the non-establishment of the financial institutions by the African Union is the bane of economic cooperation in Africa. Without the institutions, the envisaged harmonious and balanced development among member states will remain a mirage. It is submitted that for there to be effective implementation of the objectives of the African Economic Community as contained in the Abuja Treaty, there must be renewed commitment by the African leaders.

Though the African Union is said to be relatively young, the positive impacts of its activities on the citizenry are not visible. The high expectations African citizens had when the Union came into existence with handful of sound and messianic promises are gradually eroding away. The African leaders must rise up to the challenges facing the continent without fear or favour, if they really want to put Africa on the path of globalization.

Having considered or examined the African Union's economic framework, it is clear that the Union in its one decade of existence remains to a large extent, less active. This could be that since the Union is still "young" it will take a gradual approach for the institutions to be strengthened. On the other hand, lack of commitment on the part of African leaders affects the Union's performance greatly. This then calls to question the issue of whether or not the Union's objectives are achievable in the near future. Strong economic institutions and policies in the continent will accelerate the development and progress of Africa.

CHAPTER SEVEN

European Union as a Model for Regional Organisations

n considering this chapter, reliance will heavily be placed on the works of other authors within European jurisdiction and their contributions are highly acknowledged and appreciated.

European Union (EU), international organisation comprising 28 European countries and governing common economic, social, and security policies. Originally confined to western Europe, the EU undertook a robust expansion into central and eastern Europe in the early 21st century. The EU's members are Austria, Belgium, Bulgaria, Croatia, Cyprus, the Czech Republic, Denmark, Estonia, Finland, France, Germany, Greece, Hungary, Ireland, Italy, Latvia, Lithuania, Luxembourg, Malta, the Netherlands, Poland, Portugal, Romania, Slovakia, Slovenia, Spain, Sweden, and the United Kingdom. The EU was created by the Maastricht Treaty, which entered into force on November 1, 1993. The treaty was designed to enhance European political and economic integration by creating a single currency (the euro), a unified foreign and security policy, and common citizenship rights and by advancing cooperation in the areas of immigration, asylum, and judicial affairs. The EU was awarded the Nobel Prize for Peace in 2012, in recognition of the organisation's efforts to promote peace and democracy in Europe.

Origins

The EU represents one in a series of efforts to integrate Europe since World War II. At the end of the war, several western European countries sought closer economic, social, and political ties to achieve economic growth and military security and to promote a lasting reconciliation between France and Germany. To this end, in 1951 the leaders of six countries—Belgium, France, Italy, Luxembourg, the Netherlands, and West Germany—signed the Treaty of Paris, thereby, when it took effect in 1952, founding the European Coal and Steel Community (ECSC). (The United Kingdom had been invited to join the ECSC and in 1955 sent a representative to observe discussions about its ongoing development, but the Labour government of Clement Attlee declined membership, owing perhaps to a variety of factors, including the illness of key ministers, a desire to maintain economic independence, and a failure to grasp the community's impending significance.) The ECSC created a free-trade area for several key economic and military resources: coal, coke, steel, scrap, and iron ore. To manage the ECSC, the treaty established several supranational institutions: a High Authority to administrate, a Council of Ministers to legislate, a Common Assembly to formulate policy, and a Court of Justice to interpret the treaty and to resolve related disputes. A series of further international treaties and treaty revisions based largely on this model led eventually to the creation of the EU.

Creation of the European Economic Community

On March 25, 1957, the six ECSC members signed the two Treaties of Rome that established the European Atomic Energy Community (Euratom)—which was designed to facilitate cooperation in atomic energy development, research, and utilization—and the European Economic Community (EEC). The

EEC created a common market that featured the elimination of most barriers to the movement of goods, services, capital, and labour, the prohibition of most public policies or private agreements that inhibit market competition, a common agricultural policy (CAP), and a common external trade policy.

The treaty establishing the EEC required members to eliminate or revise important national laws and regulations. In particular, it fundamentally reformed tariff and trade policy by abolishing all internal tariffs by July 1968. It also required that governments eliminate national regulations favouring domestic industries and cooperate in areas in which they traditionally had acted independently, such as international trade (i.e., trade with countries outside the EEC). The treaty called for common rules on anticompetitive and monopolistic behaviour and for common inland transportation and regulatory standards. Recognizing social policy as a fundamental component of economic integration, the treaty also created the European Social Fund, which was designed to enhance job opportunities by facilitating workers' geographic and occupational mobility.

Significantly, the treaty's common market reforms did not extend to agriculture. The CAP, which was implemented in 1962 and which became the costliest and most controversial element of the EEC and later the EU, relied on state intervention to protect the living standards of farmers, to promote agricultural self-sufficiency, and to ensure a reliable supply of products at reasonable prices.

Like the ECSC, the EEC established four major governing institutions: a commission, a ministerial council, an assembly, and a court. To advise the Commission and the Council of Ministers on a broad range of social and economic policies, the treaty created an Economic and Social Committee. In 1965 members of the EEC signed the Brussels Treaty, which merged the commissions of the EEC and Euratom and the High Authority of the ECSC into a single commission. It also combined the councils of the three organizations into a common Council of Ministers. The EEC, Euratom, and the ECSC—collectively referred to as the European Communities—later became the principal institutions of the EU.

The Commission (officially known as the European Commission) consists of a permanent civil service directed by commissioners. It has had three primary functions: to formulate community policies, to monitor compliance with community decisions, and to oversee the execution of community law. Initially, commissioners were appointed by members to renewable four-year terms, which were later extended to five years. The Commission is headed by a president, who is selected by the heads of state or heads of government of the organization's members. In consultation with member governments, the president appoints the heads of the Directorate-Generals, which manage specific areas such as agriculture, competition, the environment, and regional policy. The Commission has shared its agenda-setting role with the European Council (not to be confused with the Council of Europe, an organization that is not an EU body), which consists of the leaders of all member countries. Established in 1974, the European Council meets at least twice a year to define the long-term agenda for European political and economic integration. The European Council is led by a president, an office that originally rotated among the heads of state or heads of government of member countries every six months. Upon the adoption of the Lisbon Treaty in 2009, the presidency was made permanent, with the officeholder being selected by European Council members. The president of the European Council serves a term of two and a half years—renewable once— and functions as the "face" of the EU in policy matters. The first "president of the EU," as the office came to be known, was former Belgian prime minister Herman Van Rompuy.

The main decision-making institution of the EEC and the European Community (as the EEC was renamed in 1993) and the EU has been the Council of the European Union (originally the Council of Ministers), which consists of ministerial representatives. The composition of the council changes frequently, as governments send different representatives depending on the policy area under discussion. All community legislation requires the approval of the council. The president of the council, whose office rotates among council members every six months, manages the legislative agenda. Council meetings are chaired by a minister from the country that currently holds the presidency. The exception to this rule is the Foreign Affairs Council, which, since the ratification of the Lisbon Treaty, is under the permanent supervision of the EU high representative for foreign affairs and security policy.

The Common Assembly, renamed the European Parliament in 1962, originally consisted of delegates from national parliaments. Beginning in 1979, members were elected directly to five-year terms. The size of members' delegations varies depending on population. The Parliament is organised into transnational party groups based on political ideology—e.g., the Party of European Socialists, the European People's Party, the European Federation of Green Parties, and the European Liberal, Democrat and Reform Party. Until 1987 the legislature served only as a consultative body, though in 1970 it was given joint decision-making power (with the Council of Ministers) over community expenditures.

The European Court of Justice (ECJ) interprets community law, settles conflicts between the organisation's institutions, and determines whether members have fulfilled their treaty obligations. Each member selects one judge, who serves a renewable six-year term; to increase efficiency, after the accession of 10 additional countries in 2004 the ECJ was allowed to sit in a "grand chamber" of only 13 judges. Eight impartial advocates-general assist the ECJ by presenting opinions on cases before the court. In 1989 an additional court, the Court of First Instance, was established to assist with the community's increasing caseload. The ECJ has established two important legal doctrines. First, European law has "direct effect," which means that treaty provisions and legislation are directly binding on individual citizens, regardless of whether their governments have modified national laws accordingly. Second, community law has "supremacy" over national law in cases where the two conflict. The promulgation of the Lisbon Treaty signalled the acceptance of these legal doctrines by national courts, and the ECJ has acquired a supranational legal authority.

Throughout the 1970s and '80s the EEC gradually expanded both its membership and its scope. In 1973 the United Kingdom, Denmark, and Ireland were admitted, followed by Greece in 1981 and Portugal and Spain in 1986. (The United Kingdom had applied for membership in the EEC in 1963 and in 1966, but its application was vetoed by French Pres. Charles de Gaulle.) The community's common external trade policy generated pressure for common foreign and development policies, and in the early 1970s the European Political Cooperation (EPC; renamed the Common Foreign and Security Policy by the Maastricht Treaty), consisting of regular meetings of the foreign ministers of each country, was established to coordinate foreign policy. In 1975 the European Regional Development Fund was created to address regional economic disparities and to provide additional resources to Europe's most deprived areas. In the same year, members endorsed the Lomé Convention, a development-assistance package and preferential-trade agreement with numerous African, Caribbean, and Pacific countries. Members also made several attempts to manage their exchange rates collectively, resulting in the establishment of the European Monetary System in 1979.

Single European Act

The Single European Act (SEA), which entered into force on July 1, 1987, significantly expanded the EEC's scope. It gave the meetings of the EPC a legal basis, and it called for more intensive coordination of foreign policy among members, though foreign policy decisions were made outside community institutions. The agreement brought the European Regional Development Fund formally into the community's treaties as part of a new section on economic and social cohesion that aimed to encourage the development of economically depressed areas. As a result of the act, there was a substantial increase in funding for social and regional programs. The SEA also required the community's economic policies to incorporate provisions for the protection of the environment, and it provided for a common research and technological-development policy, which was aimed primarily at funding transnational research efforts.

More generally, the SEA set out a timetable for the completion of a common market. A variety of legal, technical, fiscal, and physical barriers continued to limit the free movement of goods, labour, capital, and services. For example, differences in national health and safety standards for consumer goods were a potential impediment to trade. To facilitate the completion of the common market by 1992, the community's legislative process was modified. Originally, the Commission proposed legislation, the Parliament was consulted, and the Council of Ministers made a final decision. The council's decisions generally needed unanimity, a requirement that gave each member a veto over all legislation. The SEA introduced qualified majority voting for all legislation related to the completion of the common market. Under this system, each member was given multiple votes, the number of which depended on national population, and approval of legislation required roughly two-thirds of the votes of all members. The new procedure also increased the role of the European Parliament. Specifically, legislative proposals that were rejected by the Parliament could be adopted by the Council of Ministers only by a unanimous vote.

The Maastricht Treaty

The Maastricht Treaty (formally known as the Treaty on European Union), which was signed on February 7, 1992, created the European Union. The treaty met with substantial resistance in some countries. In Denmark, for example, voters who were worried about infringements upon their country's sovereignty defeated a referendum on the original treaty in June 1992, though a revised treaty was approved the following May. Voters in France narrowly approved the treaty in September, and in July 1993 British Prime Minister John Major was forced to call a vote of confidence in order to secure its passage. An amended version of the treaty officially took effect on November 1, 1993.

The treaty consisted of three main pillars: the European Communities, a common foreign and security policy, and enhanced cooperation in home (domestic) affairs and justice. The treaty changed the name of the European Economic Community to the European Community (EC), which became the primary component of the new European Union. The agreement gave the EC broader authority, including formal control of community policies on development, education, public health, and consumer protection and an increased role in environmental protection, social and economic cohesion, and technological research. It also established EU citizenship, which entailed the right of EU citizens to vote and to run for office in local and European Parliament elections in their country of residence, regardless of national citizenship.

The Maastricht Treaty specified an agenda for incorporating monetary policy into the EC and formalised planning that had begun in the late 1980s to replace national currencies with a common currency managed by common monetary institutions. The treaty defined a set of "convergence criteria" that specified the conditions under which a member would qualify for participation in the common currency. Countries were required to have annual budget deficits not exceeding 3 percent of gross domestic product (GDP), public debt under 60 percent of GDP, inflation rates within 1.5 percent of the three lowest inflation rates in the EU, and exchange-rate stability. The members that qualified were to decide whether to proceed to the final stage—the adoption of a single currency. The decision required the establishment of permanent exchange rates and, after a transition period, the replacement of national currencies with the common currency, called the euro. Although several countries failed to meet the convergence criteria (e.g., in Italy and Belgium public debt exceeded 120 percent of GDP), the Commission qualified nearly all members for monetary union, and on January 1, 1999, 11 countries—Austria, Belgium, Finland, France, Germany, Ireland, Italy, Luxembourg, the Netherlands, Portugal, and Spain—adopted the currency and relinquished control over their exchange rates. Greece failed to qualify, and Denmark, Sweden, and the United Kingdom chose not to apply for membership. Greece was admitted to the euro beginning in 2001. Initially used only by financial markets and businesses, the euro was introduced for use by the general public on January 1, 2002.

The Maastricht Treaty significantly modified the EEC's institutions and decision-making processes. The Commission was reformed to increase its accountability to the Parliament. Beginning in 1995, the term of office for commissioners, who now had to be approved by the Parliament, was lengthened to five years to correspond to the terms served by members of the Parliament. The ECJ was granted the authority to impose fines on members for noncompliance. Several new institutions were created, including the European Central Bank, the European System of Central Banks, and the European Monetary Institute. The treaty also created a regional committee, which served as an advisory body for commissioners and the Council of Ministers on issues relevant to subnational, regional, or local constituencies.

One of the most radical changes was the reform of the legislative process. The range of policies subject to qualified majority voting in the Council of Ministers was broadened. The treaty also endowed the Parliament with a limited right of rejection over legislation in most of the areas subject to qualified majority voting, and in a few areas, including citizenship, it was given veto power. The treaty formally incorporated the Court of Auditors, which was created in the 1970s to monitor revenue and expenditures, into the EC.

As part of the treaty's second pillar, members undertook to define and implement common foreign and security policies. Members agreed that, where possible, they would adopt common defence policies, which would be implemented through the Western European Union, a security organisation that includes many EU members. Joint actions—which were not subject to monitoring or enforcement by the Commission or the ECJ—required unanimity.

The EU's third pillar included several areas of common concern related to the free movement of people within the EU's borders. The elimination of border controls conflicted with some national immigration, asylum, and residency policies and made it difficult to combat crime and to apply national civil codes uniformly, thus creating the need for new Europe-wide policies. For example, national asylum policies that treated third-country nationals differently could not, in practice, endure once people were allowed to move freely across national borders.

Enlargement and post-Maastricht reforms

On January 1, 1995, Sweden, Austria, and Finland joined the EU, leaving Iceland, Norway, and Switzerland as the only major western European countries outside the organisation. Norway's government twice (1972 and 1994) attempted to join, but its voters rejected membership on each occasion. Switzerland tabled its application in the early 1990s. Norway, Iceland, and the members of the EU (along with Liechtenstein) are members of a free trade area called the European Economic Area, which allows freedom of movement for goods, services, capital, and people.

Two subsequent treaties revised the policies and institutions of the EU. The first, the Treaty of Amsterdam, was signed in 1997 and entered into force on May 1, 1999. Building on the social protocol of the Maastricht Treaty, it identified as EU objectives the promotion of employment, improved living and working conditions, and proper social protection; added sex-discrimination protections and transferred asylum, immigration, and civil judicial policy to the community's jurisdiction; granted the Council of Ministers the power to penalize members for serious violations of fundamental human rights; and gave the Parliament veto power over a broad range of EC policies as well as the power to reject the European Council's nominee for president of the Commission.

A second treaty, the Treaty of Nice, was signed in 2001 and entered into force on February 1, 2003. Negotiated in preparation for the admission of new members from eastern Europe, it contained major reforms. The maximum number of seats on the Commission was set at 27, the number of commissioners appointed by members was made the same at one each, and the president of the Commission was given greater independence from national governments. Qualified majority voting in the Council of Ministers was extended to several new areas. Approval of legislation by qualified voting required the support of members representing at least 62 percent of the EU population and either the support of a majority of members or a supermajority of votes cast. Although national vetoes remained in areas such as taxation and social policy, countries choosing to pursue further integration in limited areas were not precluded from doing so.

After the end of the Cold War, many of the former communist countries of eastern and central Europe applied for EU membership. However, their relative lack of economic development threatened to hinder their full integration into EU institutions. To address this problem, the EU considered a stratified system under which subsets of countries would participate in some components of economic integration (e.g., a free trade area) but not in others (e.g., the single currency). Turkey, at the periphery of Europe, also applied for membership, though its application was controversial because it was a predominantly Islamic country, because it was widely accused of human rights violations, and because it had historically tense relations with

Greece (especially over Cyprus). Despite opposition from those who feared that expansion of the EU would stifle consensus and inhibit the development of Europe-wide foreign and security policies, the EU in 2004 admitted 10 countries (Cyprus, the Czech Republic, Estonia, Hungary, Latvia, Lithuania, Malta, Poland, Slovakia, and Slovenia), all but two of which (Cyprus and Malta) were former communist states; Bulgaria and Romania joined in 2007. Negotiations on Turkey's membership application began in 2005 but faced numerous difficulties.

Building on the limited economic and political goals of the ECSC, the countries of western Europe have achieved an unprecedented level of integration and cooperation. The degree of legal integration, supranational political authority, and economic integration in the EU greatly surpasses that of other international organisations. Indeed, although the EU has not replaced the nation-state, its institutions have increasingly resembled a parliamentary democratic political system at the supranational level.

In 2002 the Convention on the Future of Europe, chaired by former French president Valéry Giscard d'Estaing, was established to draft a constitution for the enlarged EU. Among the most difficult problems confronting the framers of the document was how to distribute power within the EU between large and small members and how to adapt the organisation's institutions to accommodate a membership that would be more than four times larger than that of the original EEC. The framers also needed to balance the ideal of deeper integration against the goal of protecting members' national traditions. The drafting process evoked considerable controversy, particularly over the question of whether the constitution should mention God and the Christian heritage of much of European society (the final version did not). The proposed constitution was signed in 2004 but required ratification by all EU members to take effect; voters in France and the Netherlands rejected it in 2005, thereby scuttling the constitution at least in the short term. It would have created a full-time president, a European foreign minister, a public prosecutor, and a charter of fundamental rights. Under the constitution the powers of the European Parliament would have been greatly expanded and the EU given a "legal personality" that entailed the sole right to negotiate most treaties on its members' behalf.

Under the leadership of Germany, work began in early 2007 on a reform treaty intended to replace the failed constitution. The resulting Lisbon Treaty, signed in December 2007, required approval by all 27 EU member countries in order to take effect. The treaty, which retained portions of the draft constitution, would establish an EU presidency, consolidate foreign policy representation for the EU, and devolve additional powers to the European Commission, the European Court of Justice, and the European Parliament. Unlike the draft constitution, the Lisbon Treaty would amend rather than replace existing treaties. The treaty failed, at least in the short term, in June 2008 after it was rejected by voters in a national referendum in Ireland. However, in a second referendum, in October 2009, Irish voters—apparently concerned that another "no" vote would imperil Ireland's ailing economy—overwhelmingly approved the treaty. A week after the Irish vote, Poland completed its ratification of the treaty as well. At that time the treaty remained to be ratified by only one country, the Czech Republic. Although the Czech Parliament already had approved the treaty, Czech Pres. Václav Klaus expressed concern that it would threaten Czech sovereignty and refused to sign it. In early November, after the Czech Constitutional Court ruled that the treaty did not imperil the Czech constitution, Klaus reluctantly endorsed the document, completing the country's ratification process. Having been approved by all 27 member countries, the treaty entered into force on December 1, 2009.

Overview of the European Union at work and its major achievements

For many years, the EU institutions have been thought of as a huge bureaucracy far removed from citizens' daily lives and concerns. Yet the EU deals with issues which are critical for all Europeans.

Examples include efforts to develop liberty, prosperity, education, peace, security, justice, the protection of the environment and health, thereby helping to disseminate basic human values at the global level.

The euro: the most visible and concrete expression of the European project

Euro notes and coins have, quite successfully, been in circulation since 1 January 2002. The single currency creates a sentiment of involvement among citizens by giving them a visible, concrete example of the European project at work. An added benefit is a stable economic climate which encourages trade and growth, as well increased competitiveness for EU products and service.

There are 17 Member States in the euro zone: Austria, Belgium, Cyprus, Estonia, Finland, France, Germany, Greece, Ireland, Italy, Luxembourg, Malta, the Netherlands, Portugal, Slovakia, Slovania and Spain.

To date, the other EU Member States have not yet adopted the single European currency.

Specific result:

The euro, represented by the "€" symbol, makes it easier to travel throughout Europe and to compare prices without having to contend with uncertainties regarding exchange rates. The management of the euro is aimed at creating a stable currency with low inflation and low interest rates that promotes healthy state finances. Historically speaking, the goal of the euro project was to eliminate internal monetary competitiveness between the EU Member States by means of a unified monetary policy and economic convergence. The common currency was also a logical complement to the fulfilment of a single market. This is because a common currency increases price transparency and eliminates exchange rate fees. But it goes beyond the single market: the euro stimulates international trade, offers increased protection against external economic shocks and gives the EU a more forceful voice in world affairs.

The euro crisis: continuing to build on the fulfilment of the Economic and Monetary Union

In the midst of the current economic and financial crisis, which has had its effect on the euro as well, its many benefits are often forgotten. The financial crisis of 2007 laid bare the imperfections of the euro project and put pressure on the budgets of Member States, which were forced to avert the failure of their banks. This is why Member States undertook measures designed to improve economic policy, financial policy and budget policy within the EU - and in particular within the Eurozone:

- The **Stability and Growth Pact** was strengthened by the so-called "Treaty on Stability, Coordination and Governance in the Economic and Monetary Union", which has been in force since 1 January 2013. The Treaty imposed a specific set of criteria on the budgets of Member

151

States. Six different legislative measures were also taken, the so-called "Sixpack", which makes the Stability and Growth Pact stronger and more enforceable and which strengthens macroeconomic oversight of the Member States. For Eurozone Member States, there were two additional measures taken (the "Twopack") that provide for additional coordination and monitoring of the budgetary processes for all countries belonging to the Eurozone.

- With the "European Semester", an annual **policy coordination** framework was created for an individual Member State's economic policy. This is aimed at two issues: the identification and combating of macroeconomic imbalances that exist between the different Member States, and the supervision of budget policy.

- Finally, in addition to the convergence of economic policy and the consolidation of tax policy, work is also being done on a **banking union.** Since September 2012, work has been underway on the creation of a "Single Supervisory Mechanism" for all European banks under the direction of the European Central Bank (ECB). This is the first step towards a fully integrated banking union alongside the development of other components, such as a set of single rules, a common deposit protection scheme and a uniform dispute settlement mechanism. The proposals relate to:

A free area

One of the EU's greatest success stories was rounded off in 1993 with the full entry into force of the internal market (free movement of people, goods, services and capital).

Specific results:

- People, goods, services, capital and, to a great extent, services, can move freely within the European Union as if they were in the same country.
- Individuals can travel across most borders without any formality and it has become much easier to work, holiday or study in another EU Member State.
- Citizens all have a similar EU passport.
- Consumers have access to a greater range of goods and service and comparing prices is easier since the introduction of the euro.

Peace and stability in Europe and throughout the entire world

Having learned the lessons from the armed conflicts of the early 20th century (the first and second World Wars) and more recent hostilities (in ex-Yugoslavia and Kosovo) which took place on its soil, Europe has taken a resolute stance to promote peace and stability both within its own borders and at the global level.

This is first and foremost achieved by promoting human rights, democracy and active diplomacy focussing on conflict prevention, and the reason why the EU has developed a Common Foreign and Security Policy (CFSP).

Similarly, the EU also aims to build a genuine common European Security and Defence Policy (CSDP) to protect EU territory and carry out peacekeeping missions.

Specific result:

- Since 2003, the EU is capable of deploying a European combat force of about 60,000 troops. This combat force can act either independently or in conjunction with NATO units. This has enabled the EU to launch civilian and military crisis management operations in the Balkans (Former Yugoslav Republic of Macedonia and Bosnia-Herzegovina), Africa (Democratic Republic of the Congo) and Afghanistan.

- The system of "EU Battle groups" (EUBG) was developed, which makes it possible to instantly deploy approximately 1,500 troops at any time (within 15 days) in the event of an international crisis. A group of EU Member States take turns maintaining troops on standby for this purpose.

- The singular fulfilment of peace on the European continent is recognised all over the world. In 2012, the European Union was awarded the Nobel Peace Prize for its successful commitment to peace, reconciliation, democracy and human rights in Europe.

- The most successful foreign policy initiative of the European Union is unquestionably its geographic expansion. Countries wishing to become a member of the EU must comply with an extensive list of conditions, which includes respect for democracy, human rights and the rule of law. With its expansions of 2004 and 2007, the Union demonstrated its unique capacity for effecting peaceful and democratic transition by admitting ten formerly communist countries. This same transitional process is now taking shape for the countries of the Western Balkans.

Europe 2020: a ten-year plan for growth in the European Union

"Europe 2020", or the EU 2020 strategy, is a long-term strategy of the European Union that was adopted by the European Council of 17 June 2010. The goal of Europe 2020 is, on the one hand, to overcome the economic crisis, but also to address and to make adjustments to the structural problems of the European growth model. In this context, the European economy must be developed into a more competitive, social and green market economy. It builds on the Lisbon strategy, which was in effect until 2010 and also had a duration of ten years.

The strategy formulates ambitious targets in five areas (employment, innovation, education, social inclusion and climate/energy), targets that the EU is seeking to attain by 2020. Three core initiatives were also formulated to address young people, skills and jobs, and the combating of poverty and social marginalisation.

The concrete measures that countries are required to undertake in order to fulfil the Lisbon strategy are also monitored within the scope of the European Semester for policy coordination. It is only when Member States act purposefully and when their measures are properly coordinated with each other that the desired results can be achieved.

A unique area of Freedom, Security and Justice

One of the EU's priorities (which has been given added weight in the European Constitution) is to guarantee Europeans a unique area of freedom, security and justice. All too often, the authority of police services and courts is limited to their national territory while crime and terrorism do not stop at a country's borders.

For this reason, the European Union decided to take a series of common measures to effectively combat these scourges in all Member States. These measures include more effective protection of basic individual rights, promoting initiatives in the field of European citizenship and a common policy for managing migration flows, developing a common European asylum policy and judicial cooperation in civil matters, promoting a coherent prosecution policy and intensifying the fight against terrorism.

Specific results:

- With regard to crime, national police forces are working more closely together, notably through Europol. Databases make it possible to gather, analyse and share information on criminal activities.
- With regard to terrorism, the attacks of 11 September 2001 in the United States prompted the Members States to pass laws ensuring a certain level of consistency in the definition of acts of terrorism and for sentencing measures.
- With regard to justice, citizens must be able to call on the courts and authorities of all Members States as easily as they would in their own country. For example, rulings and decisions must be complied with and implemented in all EU countries, the goal being greater compatibility and convergence among the various Member States' legal systems.

A common Commercial Policy

The common commercial policy, which is based on the Member States' Customs Union, includes common arrangements for imports as well as a common external tariff uniformly applied to all Member States.

The policy's objective is to contribute to the harmonious development of world trade and the reduction of customs barriers. It has been clearly shown that free trade based on fair rules is beneficial to stability and development not only for the EU, but also far beyond its borders. Through the common commercial policy, EU countries take part in trade negotiations as a single group and thereby further promote Europe's image throughout the world.

Efforts are also made to bear in mind the poorest countries when developing the EU's common commercial policy, although they often accuse it of refusing to let in more of their exports, particularly agricultural products. Nevertheless, in its Generalised System of Preferences (GSP) the EU grants duty-free access or preferential access at a reduced rate to its market for certain imports from developing countries or economies in transition. Exports from the world's 49 poorest countries (with the exception of weapons) have also been granted duty-free access to the European market.

Specific result:
• Products entering the EU are charged the same duties regardless of whether they are imported, for example, via the port of Antwerp or via the port of Athens.

A common agricultural policy

The European Union set up the Common Agricultural Policy (CAP) to increase agricultural productivity, provide for an adequate standard of living for agricultural workers, stabilise markets, guarantee security of supply and ensure reasonable prices for consumers. While maintaining these initial objectives, the most recent CAP reforms also take account of growing societal concerns regarding food safety and quality, environmental protection issues and animal welfare.

Specific result:
• From now on, payments of direct aid to farmers will be contingent on compliance with food safety, environmen-

tal and animal health and welfare standards, in addition to the application of good agricultural practices. Through its rural development programmes, the CAP also makes an essential contribution to boosting the competitiveness of agriculture, improving the rural environment and spaces and diversifying economic activities in rural areas. Compliance with European legislation stemming from the common agricultural policy is the responsibility of various verification bodies at both the federal and regional level.

A social Europe and the unified policy

Social considerations continue to play an important role in the European project. Through its Directives, the EU aims to arrive at a convergence between the laws of Member States in fields such as employment, social protection and working conditions to develop a common, basic set of rules at the European level. The Treaty of Lisbon strengthens the social policy of the European Union by explicitly incorporating its social values into its founding treaties and by formulating new social attainment targets. Social policy, however, belongs to the shared powers of the EU and its Member States. This means that its concrete development and implementation occurs mainly at the level of the Member States.

To do this, the EU has developed measures to encourage convergence and advocates coordination methods between Members States.

With regard to employment and growth, the EU actively tries to involve the social partners in order to ensure that the interests of all parties are adequately represented.

Lastly, solidarity in Europe is also the cohesion policy, which aims to gradually work away development shortcomings or stimulate conversions in certain regions of the EU.

Specific results:

- the free movement of workers and the coordination of social security systems: all EU nationals are entitled to work, without any discrimination, in another Members State and to benefit from its social insurance system;
- gender equality: five Directives have been issued since 1975 to guarantee equal treatment at work, the same salary for the same job and access to social security cover;
- labour law: protection of individual and collective rights and a guarantee of safety and security in the workplace;
- the fight against various forms of discrimination;
- several Belgian provinces have benefitted from EU funds to support their development initiatives or to assist in their economic conversion (specifically Hainaut, Liege, Limburg and Antwerp).

Environment and health: our problem children

Taking care of the environment to safeguard quality of life for current and future generations is one of the EU's main priorities, and it has embarked on the ambitious project to combine environmental protection and economic growth. The main priorities are as follows: preventing climate change and fighting global warming, protecting nature areas and the wild flora and fauna, dealing with health and environmental problems and finding better waste management solutions.

Clearly, very many environmental problems go far beyond the EU's borders and this is why it has signed international programmes and conventions tackling problems such as acid rain, biodiversity, climate change and greenhouse gases.

Specific results:
- The Ecolabel scheme helps European consumers make more eco-friendly choices when selecting products or services;
- The European Environment Agency monitors the state of the environment and issues alerts when problems are detected. This in turn makes it possible for the EU to take the necessary legislative measures;
- The well-known Kyoto protocol (greenhouse gas reduction) was in part initiated by the EU, which remains one its most fervent proponents, and it symbolises the beginning of global awareness of the risk of climate change;
- In the 1990s, the EU decided to require catalytic converters on all vehicles and to stop adding lead to petrol.
- In 2007, the European Union formulated three targets (the 20-20-20 plan) to be attained by 2020 (relative to 1990 levels): a 20% reduction in CO_2 emissions (if an agreement can be reached on a global climate treaty, the EU will commit to increasing this target to 30%), a 20% reduction in energy consumption, and 20% of total energy consumption derived from renewable energy.

A knowledge-based society

The European Union has set itself the objective of becoming the most competitive and dynamic knowledge-based society in the world. As a result, education, professional training and support for young people have become three major priority areas.

Every year, thousands of European citizens benefit from cross-border education or training programmes which foster intercultural understanding and make it possible to live, study, specialise and work in other European countries.

Educational qualifications are accredited in other EU countries and citizens' access to training, whether in their own country or another Member State, is made easier through partnerships, exchange programmes and the elimination of numerous administrative hurdles.

Specific results:

The European Union provides a wide range of training and educational programmes, which beginning in 2014 will fall under the umbrella of a single, larger programme known as "Erasmus for All". All previous programmes for education and training or youth and sport (such as Erasmus, Leonardo da Vinci, Comenius Grundtvig or Youth in Action) will be integrated into this larger program. The best-known component of this is undoubtedly the Erasmus programme for the exchange of students and teachers between European universities.

In 2011, approximately 250,000 young people studied or fulfilled traineeships abroad thanks to this programme. The Erasmus for All programme provides support for three types of activities: learning opportunities both inside and outside the EU (studies, training programmes, traineeships, etc.); institutional cooperation between educational institutions, governments, youth organisations and companies; and support for policy reforms in the Member States and cooperation with countries outside the EU.

European Union (EU): History, Members, Aims and Achievements of EEC

Smriti Chand on his part looks at European Union in this perspective:

The European Union (EU) is supranational and intergovernmental union of 27 states in Europe. It was established in 1992 by the Treaty on European Union (The Maastricht Treaty) and is the de facto successor to the six-member European Economic Community founded in 1957.

Since then new accessions have raised its number of member states and competencies have expanded. The EU is the current stage of a continuing open-ended process of European integration.

The EU is one of the largest economic and political entities in the world, with 494 million peoples and a combined nominal Gross Domestic Product (GDP) of £11.6 ($14.5) trillion in 2006. The Union is the single market with a common trade policy, a Common Agriculture/Fisheries Policy and a Regional Policy to assist underdeveloped regions.

It introduced a single currency, the euro, adopted by 13 member states. The EU imitated a limited Common Foreign and Security Policy and a limited Police and Judicial Co-operation in Criminal Matters.

Important EU institutions and bodies include the European Commission, the Council of the European Union, the European Council, the European Central Bank, the European Court of Justice and the European Parliament.

Citizens of EU member states are also EU citizens they directly elect the European Parliament, once every five years. They can live, travel, work and invest in other members states (with some restrictions on new member states). Passport control and customs checks at most internal borders were abolished by the Schengen Agreement.

History:

The EU has evolved from a western European trade body into the supranational and intergovernmental body. After the Second World War, an impetus grew in western European for institutional forms of cooperation (through social, political and economic integration) between states, driven by the determination to rebuild European and eliminate the possibility of another war between Germany and France. Eastern European, on the other hand, was largely within the soviet sphere of influence and only in the 1990s did was the EU see central and eastern European states as potential members.

In 1976 Winston Church-chill called for a "United States of European" (though without the inclusion of the UK). On 9 May 1950 the French foreign minister Robert Schuman presented a proposal for the joint management if France's and West Germany's coal and steel industries.

The proposal, known as the "Schuman Declaration", envisaged the scheme as "the first concrete step towards a European federation". It is considered to be the beginning of the creation of what in now the European Union and led to the formation of the European Coal and steel community by West Germany, France, Italy and the Benelux countries. This was accomplished by the Treaty of Paris, signed in 1951. The founding nations singing the Treaty of Rome in 1957.

The first full customs union, the European Economic Community, was established by the Treaty of Rome in 1957 and implemented on 1st January 1958. This later changed to the European Community, which is now the "first pillar" European Union created by the Maastricht treaty.

On 29 October 2004, EU member state heads of government and state signed the Treaty establishing the Constitution for European. This was later ratified by 17 member states. However, in most cases ratification was based on parliamentary action, rather than popular vote and the process faltered on 29 May, 2005 when French voters rejected the constitution by 55% to 45%. The French rejection was followed three days later by a Dutch one, in which 62% of voters rejected the constitution as well.

European Economic Community (EEC):

A prominent policy goal of the European Union is the development and maintenance of an effective single market. Significant efforts have been made to create harmonized standards claimed by their proponents to bring economic benefits through creating larger, more efficient markets.

Since the Treaty of Rome, policies have implemented free trade of goods and services among member states and continue to do so. This policy goal was further extended to three of the four European Free Trade Association (EFTA) states by the European Economic Area, (EEA).

Common EU competition law restricts anti¬competitive activities of companies (through antitrust law and merger control) and member states (through the State Aids regime). The EU promotes free movement of capital between member states (and other EEA states). The members have a common system of indirect taxation, the Value Added Tax (VAT), as well as common customs duties and excises on various products.

From 2007 to 2013 new member states expect investments financed with EU Structural Funds and Cohesion Funds, (new motorway near Poznan, Poland) they have a Common Agriculture Policy (with the Common Fisheries Policy) and the structural and cohesion funds, which improve infrastructure and assist disadvantaged regions. Together they are known as the cohesion polices.

The EU also has funds for emergency financial aid, for instance after natural disaster. The funding extends to programmes in candidate countries and other East European countries, as well as aid to many developing countries, through programmes. The EU also funds research and technological development, thorough four-year Framework Programmes for Research and Technological Development.

In a more political sense, the EU attempts to create with much controversy a sense of European citizenship and European political life. That includes freedom for citizens of the EU to vote and to stand as candidates in local government and European Parliament elections in any member state.

Members of EEC:

The six states that founded the EEC and the other two Communities were known as the "inner six" (the "outer seven" were those countries who formed the European Free Trade Association). The six were France, West Germany, Italy and the three Benelux countries: Belgium, the Netherlands and Luxembourg.

The first enlargement was in 1973, with the accession of Denmark, Ireland and the United Kingdom. Greece, Spain and Portugal joined throughout in the 1980s. Following the creation of the EU in 1993, it has enlarged to include a further fifteen countries by 2007.

Aims and Achievements of EEC:

The main aim of the EEC, as stated in its preamble, was to "preserve peace and liberty and to lay the foundations of an ever closer union among the peoples of Europe". Calling for balanced economic growth, this was to be accomplished through, (1) the establishment of a customs union with a common external tariff (2) common policies for agriculture, transport and trade (3) enlargement of the EEC to the rest of Europe.

For the customs union, the treaty provided for a 10 % reduction in custom duties and up to 20 % of global import quotas. Progress on the customs union proceeded much faster than the twelve years planned, however France faced some setbacks due to their war with Algeria.

Euro Currency:

Euro currency was created by the Economics and Monetary Union (EMU). It was established on 1 January 1999 and based on the Maastricht treaty from 1992. 12 countries are members of the Euro area also known as the Euroland. Every other member of the EU can join this group provided that certain conditions (regulating the level of inflation and the condition of public money etc.) are fulfilled.

But not all the EU have introduced the Euro-currency, some haven't met the requirements (Sweden isn't member of the EMU and Greece has met the requirement in 2000 and since then it has been a member of the Euro-land) and other decided that maybe they introduce Euro sometime later (UK and Denmark). Countries which jointed the EU in 2004 aren't in the Euro area.

In the beginning of 1999 member countries of EMU have lost the right to release their national currency giving this right to the European Central Bank. But why they gave this right, one of the most important privileges of sovereign countries, you may ask. The answer is simple and not clarifying anything because of political reasons.

European countries wanted to establish a new federation structure which would ensure peace and provide good economic conditions. The most important thing was to establish such, connections between Germany and other countries that no more was could outbreak.

Economic reasons were also very important in the creation of the Euro area. Since 1993 all EU countries function as a uniform market where services and products and man-power flow freely.

The process of eliminating borders between countries took a few decades and after it has finished it became obvious that what economy need was unification of currency. EU's members would no longer have to pay for exchanging national currencies and it would allow companies to save money (according to the European Council the savings would be of about 40 billion USD annually).

What Influences The Euro Exchange Rate?

Only the European Systems of Central Bank (ESCB), which works similarly as German central bank, the Bundes bank. Bundes bank is known for excellent ant-inflation policies can release Euro currency. ESCB is divided into central unit (European Central Bank (ECB) which was created on 1 June 1998) and national central banks.

The main ECB's task is take care of monetary politics and national banks realize these politics in member countries. The aim of the aforementioned politics is to maintain price stability that means keeping the inflation level below 2%. EMU's central bank can support economical growth as long as it doesn't collide with its anti-inflation ESCB's politics has to be the same in the whole Euro-land.

These politics could lead to a rise of unemployment level and escalate social conflicts. In this case the creators of Maastricht treaty have added in this treaty a few points assuring that countries' politics and economical situation would not influence bank's decisions.

The bank has the sovereignty needed to resist political pressure and to concentrate on keeping the inflation level low. All this is to make Euro currency the second (after the American dollar) one in the world.

The process of the Euro currency introduction was three and a half years long. There are many reasons for this. Technical aspects are the most important; it takes a while to print 12 billion green backs and to produce 70 billion coins.

But 300 million people and many companies would also have to get used to the new Euro Currency (you don't change a currency every day, you know). The magnitude of this undertaking caused that it was decided that it would be best to introduce Euro step-by-step.

This process is divided into two parts: transitional part; from 1 January 1999 to 31 December 2001, where there aren't any Euro notes or coins. National currencies aren't independent they have became parts of Euro. The exchange rate (1 Euro Currency = x National Currency) has been accepted by the Council of the European Union and it does not change.

From the beginning of 1999 only Euro currency does exist in the Euro-land but it is divided into certain particles. National currencies disappear from the international currency market and Euro is put in their place. Final part: from 1 January 2002 to 30 June 2002, national currencies are withdrawn from public usage and Euro greenbacks and coins are introduced.

On 1 January 2002 all savings in national currencies in banks are converted into Euro. Prices displayed only in Euro.

National currencies can be used only until the end of the final part; from 1 July 2002 Euro is the only legal currency in the Euro-land.

The introduction of Euro is one of the most important events not only in the history of Europe but also in the history of the World. A dozen European countries, altogether a huge economic potential, take part in it.

Due to their role in international trade and finances the success of this undertaking would benefit all. All necessary steps will be taken to ensure Euro's stability and functionality. Only then will Euro earn international respect as currently being touted.

CHALLENGES OF THE EUROPEAN UNION IN THE 21ST CENTURY

The European Union is a spectacular success story of the integration of European states that used to fight between each other in the past. It is considered the most advanced international organisation in the world, with supranational decision making institutions, common trade, agricultural, social policies as well as foreign and security policy tools. On one side, for some Member States it is accomplishment for dreams of stabilization and economic progress, while for others it is an obsolete institution blocking sovereignty and development with its strict regulations. What are the challenges for an EU in the 21st century, now that it has grown up to 28 member states? What are the objectives of further developing the EU, while peace and stability was already achieved? What are the main threats to the existence and wellbeing of the EU member states?

First of all, the EU in the 21st century is the world's largest economy. It is also the largest trading block with a GDP per head of €25,000 and 500 million inhabitants, gathering 28 different countries in one political, social and economic union. Regardless, it has to face a list of internal and external challenges which not answered may lead to a serious crisis. At the moment, the European Union is facing serious economic crises, caused by the global financial crisis in 2008, as well as faulty industrial policies, and, capital and labour movements on a global scale. The EU economy is becoming less competitive compared to the United States, Brazil or China. EU Member States are witnessing huge unemployment rates, especially among youth, while the labour markets have shifted towards developing countries. The single European market was launched in 1993 with success, but the 2008 crisis indicated that it didn't prevent the EU economy from turmoil. Meanwhile, EU leaders who are negotiating the Free Trade Area with the US are trying to boost common economies and fight huge unemployment. Another problem is the differences in regional development, the effectiveness of the cohesion policy, in addition to resolving issues of how competitive the EU economy is in comparison with the BRIC countries.

Secondly, the European Union is witnessing a serious political crisis, apparent in its decreasing political legitimacy and complicated decision-making policies. In the recent European Parliament elections, polls have shown the lowest turnout in the history, equal to turnout in last elections in 2009, since the first elections of 1979. This is indicative of low levels of faith EU citizens have in the European Parliament's power of changing their welfare situation. As an outcome of the crisis, European states are experiencing growing activity and support towards parties of the extreme right, who support eurosceptical populism. To this end, parties like Hungary's Jobbik, National Front of Marine Le Pen in France or Party of Geert Wilders in Netherlands have gained serious influence in the new EP. The absence of charismatic European leaders like Konrad Adenauer, Willy Brandt,

Charles de Gaulle or Jacque Delors are very well other symptoms of the political crisis in the European Union.

Thirdly, problems at the society level are emerging as a serious threat to the stability of European Union. Our societies are aging, while the lack of proper pro-natalist policies fail to encourage European families to have more children. This will undoubtedly have strong consequences in the quality of life, pensions of future generations, migration policies, and the competitiveness of entering the European Union. Among the initiatives towards creating common European citizenship, the Erasmus program remains most successful. Immigration policies in most European Union member states seems to fail and not provide appropriate codification of the law that would be beneficial for the EU economy and for potential migrants from outside the EU.

Jean Claude Piris, diplomat and politician said that "For decades, we, Europeans, have been accustomed to progress: peace, democracy, end of East-West division, improvement in economic and social prosperity, improved health standards, better protection of human rights, equality between men and women". It is apparent that these times are gone and new challenges are knocking on the EU's doors. Peace, which was so desired among European states after the war stricken time of 1945, seems to be threatened in light of the turmoil in Ukraine. The worsening condition of democracy in the European Union's decision-making structures is just another indicator of the new challenges it will face in the coming years. Ultimately, if the EU fails to implement strong economic and political solutions, it will become less competitive in the global political economy. The EU has to speak with one unanimous voice while tackling global problems, responding to the Ukraine-Russia crisis, while also being mindful of military conflicts, like the civil war in Syr-

171

ia or Israeli-Palestinian conflict. All this may confirm that the EU project has lost sight of its main objectives, and the EU needs a new European renaissance. This is the view presented by CezarySzczepaniuk in his article "Challenges of European Union in the 21st Century."

CHAPTER EIGHT

Inherent Challenges facing the Union

Introduction

Various scholars with long experience in the continent have through their works pointed out multiple factors responsible for low performance of Africa Union in carrying on the business of modernisation and consolidation of political institutions.

Many scholars had added considerable depth with thorough look at colonial and pre-colonial history with its attendant impact on the continent's progress. Key issues such as ethnicity, urbanisation, economic crisis, party politics, the military, apartheid and adverse external interferences, abound.

The secret of fast attainment of the purposes of things is in the laws by which those things were created. In other words, the law that creates a thing reveals its composition which makes possible the attainment of its highest purpose. A nation, people or community function according to the fundamental laws of their composition, and if the best is required to be attained from such nation, people or community, it is better attained through the proper manipulation of the laws of their composition. The law of a matter is what is called 'true knowledge' or the 'key of knowledge' of the matter. If the basic laws of a matter are wrong, there is no way such a matter can actually be maximally put to great use to attain its purpose.

When the fundamental laws by which things are created and managed, are actually put into operation, dominion can be achieved in all endeavours. Leaders are being referred to as those who have access to the key of knowledge, the **fundamental laws of all that is feasible in a society,** which they seem not to be using and would not allow others to use either. The use of fundamental laws is what makes **all things possible for systems.**

Near Absence of Rule of Law

It has been discovered that the problem of Africa is that its component fundamental laws or ordinances have always been jettisoned, and it has shown itself fully in almost all continental endeavours. Africa has great potentials, but it is not able to break-forth and spread-abroad in any particular area. The continent has ever since been living on potentials, possibilities and such words without actually breaking forth into the full visible attainment of the potentials. I believe that it is because most of the laws of the land are either obsolete or obeyed in abeyance. For instance, the Constitutive Act which is meant to help the member-State achieve its target, is relegated to the background and no proactive step is taken in reducing crimes such as terrorism, insurgency' political violence inter alia to the barest minimum, while those impunities threaten the life, property and peace of the population. In Nigeria and Libya the terrorists are busy taking over some parts of the territories but the governments and their security agents are doing virtually nothing to savage the situation.

Another fundamental flaw of law and justice system in Africa is that knowing the nature of Africans and how they stop at nothing to conceal their culpability or that of their relatives in criminal activities, our laws' most of them being obsolete, still consider criminals, drug lords, fraudsters, robbers, kidnappers and high crime like corruption suspects (even those under custody) as mere suspects until proven guilty by conviction in a court of law; whereas in our unique situation, it would be more suitable to go deeper or higher, just as the Chinese do, to curtail the many different escape routes such as legal technicalities employed by suspects to evade justice. Stiffer punishment to serve as deterrent to would be offenders is hereby recommended.

Poor Leadership

Transformational leadership has continued to be a major challenge. This is why many African leaders have continued to act the agency script for their masters the colonial and neo-colonial imperialist powers who laid out some of those laws to create a mental slavery to divide and rule us as victims of their imperialist manipulation and control to the point that our leaders at some point become unable to actually have a leadership mind of their own. This is akin to a pathological situation called megalomania or a psychosomatic disorder otherwise known as manic-depression which becomes emotionally entrenched in the spirit of a person in a manner that a victim has to be subjected to some exorcism or deliverance or both for him to overcome the compulsion which results in the disorderly state every now and then.

This has opened our eyes more to the glaring necessity to embark on a general reconciliation of the various positions that are at variance with the development focus of the continent to be able to come to the truth and to really make up our minds to deploy the right laws and strategies to make progress. No nation under such colonial conditioning, before or now, ever made any headway until after they have embarked on a truth commission kind of reconciliation. The ordinance or fundamental law of development requires that there must be peace for development to take place, and there can never be peace unless there is reconciliation whether it is colonial imperialist manipulation and conditioning or any other strategy used to manipulate either the poor or the less privileged. It has been seen at least in South Africa and Ghana in Africa. There are other countries that have evolved the same strategies to come to the same conclusions such as Chile, Peru, Canada and so on. The aim is always to give the country a broad and reliable picture of past abuses and crimes by its people against themselves, and to use that to re-write the history of the country to give it a better focus.

The African Union is therefore enjoined to seek to turn its General Assembly meetings into a Truth and Reconciliation Commission to reconcile the different elements of agitations, and to evolve the right kind of contributions that are worthy to fashion a good justice system that will give us a leeway to attain real development, without which our journey will continue to be a voyage of no end.

Rising Insecurity

Nigeria, for instance, which claims to be the giant of Africa is on the verge of being a failed state. Terrorism, insurgency corruption inter alia are fast ravaging the country under the very nose of the leaders who took oath to defend its constitution and integrity. Those in authority flagrantly obey the laws of the land in breach.

Service delivery laws are the most hit in this spate of flawed fundamental laws such as enabling laws in the power sector where all power to regulate the sector is the exclusive preserve of the Federal Government to the extent that even where the State Governments establish plants and produce power, they release the whole plant to the Federal Government to run and distribute (now through the appointed companies) by which the power situation has been turned into a joking matter where even States that produce the power do not see the light produced anymore as the Federal Government gives one excuse after another for failure to distribute light effectively. It is the same situation with the mining of solid minerals spread across the land, where, unless the Federal Government approves, no one can actually mine the solid minerals at industrial levels. These laws are not progressive; they do not give power to the people, rather they concentrate power in the purview of the Federal Government. To get the population performing at optimum, government should allow the regions and big establishments the express freedom to establish and distribute their own energy power, which should be based on government specifications. In this way, energy power taken away from the monopoly of government will be freely available and will generate the explosion of industries and industrial revolution

Again, to get the population performing or functioning by the strengths and capacities of its human and mineral resources means that Government system must endeavour to evolve a combination of co-ownership of all endeavours. Endeavours such as public educational schools should be owned partly by government, and the bigger part should be shared among teachers and parents in the communities located. Government should evolve industrialisation by subsidies such as is being practiced in China. Groups who propose to establish fruit juice industries in fruits-dominated communities, for instance, should receive subsidies to establish such industries and share profits between the group and the government, and this should be the standard used to compel companies to group themselves and establish in places where raw materials are in abundance.

Another area of industrial revolution and fast creation of jobs is communication, computer and telecommunication. If there is concentration of subsidies for massive activities in these sectors, in five years' time, unemployment will drastically reduce. All these endeavours are the most successful in terms of giving empowerment to the poor to produce their food and also raise the cities, should be subjected to the right fundamental laws that can establish them and actually see them have the poor empowered and able to bring transformation in the areas of food production and raising of the cities. If the youth folk of the continent is actively engaged in fruitful ventures, most of the evils bedevilling the continent will be reduced to the barest minimum.

Upsurge of Internally Displaced Persons

Man is a social animal therefore whatever he does is geared towards achieving, the social status. In recognition of the social status, over the years man has evolved ways and means to make sure that the society in which he lives gives meaning to human existence. Naturally, a man is born with innate and inalienable rights which naturally flow as a result of such birth. They are innate and inalienable because without them there cannot be human existence. Rights such as life, speech, movement or liberty among others follow man from his mother's womb and all of them are inseparable. In recognition of this, the United Nations in December, 1948 made and adopted Universal Declaration of Human Rights wherein the preamble emphasises that "recognition of the inherent dignity and of the equal and inalienable rights of the human family is the foundation of freedom, Justice and Peace in the world." "Human family" therefore presupposes the entire humanity irrespective of creed, race, place of birth or circumstance surrounding human existence.

It has been argued that the content of the principle of respect for human rights in international Law may be expressed in three propositions:

(1)   All states have a duty to respect the fundamental rights and freedoms of all persons within their territories;

(2)   states have a duty not to permit discrimination by reason of sex, race, religion or language; and

(3)   states have a duty to promote universal respect for human rights and to co-operate with each other to achieve this objective. The first proposition covers and encompasses the other two.

The United Nations Universal Declaration of Human Rights encapsulates the above propositions. In furtherance of this position, United Nations has subsequently adopted a number of Conventions with respect to promotion and protection of human rights in specific areas such as Genocide Convention, Elimination of Racial Discrimination, Convention Relating to Status of Refugees and its protocols among others.

Since regional bodies are the important components in achieving the objectives of United Nations, various Regional organisations promulgated different instruments to fulfil the UN aspiration for Universal Human Rights. African Continent through its various bodies have adopted various international and regional legal instruments with respect to promoting and protecting the rights of all members of human family including internally displaced persons (otherwise known as IDPs).

In 2009, African Union at its Special Summit held at Kampala, Uganda, adopted African Union Convention for the Protection and Assistance of Internally Displaced Persons in Africa otherwise called Kampala Convention. The preamble to the convention recognises and states in part the International and Regional Legal instruments dealing with the promotion and protection the rights of human beings irrespective of their conditions. It reads in part that: RECALLING the 1948 Universal Declaration of Human Rights, the 1948 Convention on the Prevention and Punishment of the Crime of Genocide, the 1948 Four Geneva Conventions and the 1977 Additional Protocols to the Geneva Conventions, the 1951 United Nations Convention Relating to the Status of Refugees, the 1969 OAU Convention Governing the Specific Aspects of Refugee problems in Africa, the 1979 Convention on Elimination of All Forms of Discrimination Against Women, the 1981 African Charter of Human and People's Rights and the 2003 protocol to the African Charter on Human and People's Rights on the Rights of Women in Africa, the 1990 African Charter on the Rights and Welfare of the Child, the 1994 Addis Ababa Document on Refugees and forced population Displacement in Africa, and other relevant United Nations and African Union human rights instruments, and relevant Security Council Resolutions.

The preamble to the above convention shows that since 1945 when United Nations came into being as an international institution, several attempts have been made to promote and protect the right of all members of human family without discrimination. This chapter focus mainly on the rights of IDPs under the watch of the African Union as the 'saviour' of African continent.

The failure of the Union on Protection and Assistance of Internally Displaced Persons.

The convention has a number of objectives that are worth considering. Like a beautiful bride with all her adornment, the convention has provided for fantastic objectives which, if properly harnessed, would bring tranquillity and peaceful co-existence among Africans. For the purpose of proper understanding, the objectives of the convention are to:

a. *Promote and strengthen regional and national measures to prevent or mitigate, prohibit and eliminate root causes of internal displacement as well as provide for durable solutions;*

b. *Establish a legal framework for preventing internal displacement, and protecting and assisting internally displaced persons in Africa;*

c. *Establish a legal framework for solidarity, cooperation, promotion of durable solutions and mutual support between the state parties in order to combat displacement and address its consequences;*

d. *Provide for the obligations and responsibilities of states parties, with respect to the prevention of internal displacement and protection of, and assistance, to internally displaced persons;*

e. *Provide for the respective obligations, responsibilities and roles of armed groups, non-state actors and other relevant actors, including civil society organisations, with respect to the prevention of internal displacement and protection of, and assistance to, internally displaced persons.*

Looking at these objectives in the facial appearance one would be left with no option but an inevitable conclusion that African Union means well and is up for serious business in respect of the rights of refugees or internally displaced persons. Nevertheless, line by line assessment of these objectives makes one wonder whether there has ever been commitment to the paper proclamations.

The first objective talks about promoting and strengthening regional and national measures to prevent or mitigate, prohibit and *eliminate* root causes of internal displacement as well provide *durable solutions.* It has been argued in this book earlier that African Union is like a toothless bull dog that can bark but cannot bite when it comes to enforcing its legal orders. The Union which has the right of intervention in the affairs of members states in cases of serious war crimes or genocides has persistently and consistently negated its duties and responsibilities. "National measure;" are the sole responsibility of the member states and when they fail, the Union does little or nothing in compelling them to so do. In most cases, member states who are faced with the challenge of internal displacement are left to bear the burden alone even when the union is invited to help.

Another aspect of the objective is to 'prohibit and eliminate root causes of internal displacement'. If the Union refuses to intervene in the affairs of the members, though it has right to so do, how can it prohibit and eliminate the root causes of displacement and armed conflict or provide durable solutions? Paper provisions without concomitant or proactive steps towards achieving the set objectives is a mere jamboree with resultant cacophony.

The second objective deals with establishment of legal framework for preventing internal displacement and protecting internally displaced persons. There are existing legal instruments including this convention which, if properly harnessed will serve as legal frame work for the achievement of all the objectives therein in particular and those contained in the Constitutive Act in general. The union in its over thirteen years of existence has failed to establish its judicial arm, the Court of Justice, thereby making it difficult to enforce its legal order. At the national level, there are other legal impediments that prevent individual member states from handling issues bordering on the union's legal instruments. In Nigeria, for instance, the constitutional bottleneck of domesticating all international treaties, conventions, protocols or instruments before they are given effect thereto is a great obstacle to the effective implementation of the union's legal instrument. This also applies to the third objective of the convention which predicates on establishment of legal framework for solidarity, cooperation, promotion of durable solutions...

Since the establishment of legal framework to deal with the situation appears to be weak, the achievement of objectives (d) and (e) appears to be a mirage. Though those obligations are copiously provided in the convention, the absence of strong and workable legal framework makes their realisation a day dream. No member state can be compelled by the union to comply with, and enforce those responsibilities since its legal order is virtually unenforceable. It is submitted that no matter how beautifully couched, the lack of force in the Union's legal instruments makes it an empty vessel that can only make a noise. The lack of force as a feature of a good legislation makes the convention a resolution without binding force on member states. Some analysts have posited that the objective of the convention to address and combat the problem of displacement are measures of its operationalisation. This position however, is not in tune with the modern reality.

Obligations of States Parties

The African Union Convention for Protection and Assistance of Internally Displaced Persons in Africa popularly known as Kampala Convention has 23 Articles. Article 3 of the convention deals with the general obligations relating to states parties. Article 3(1)(a) imposes obligations on states parties to refrain from, prohibit and prevent arbitrary displacement of population. This therefore means that the framers of the convention indeed knew that the state parties have one role or other to play in the displacement of the citizens. This could be through their policies or polity that affects the populace adversely. The proposition can evidently be seen in Article 12 of the convention which makes it obligatory for states parties to establish effective legal framework to provide just and fair compensation and other forms of reparations, where appropriate, to internally displaced persons for damage incurred as a result of displacement, in accordance with International standard.

Again, the convention enjoins states parties to prevent political, social, cultural and economic exclusion and marginalisation, that are likely to cause displacement of populations or persons by virtue of their social identity, religion or political opinion. A critical appraisal of the said provision brings out the salient or microscopic realities of socio-political happenings in Africa. Politics of intrigues, nepotism and the rich-get-richer as well as the poor-get-poorer dominates the African social strata as against the legal regimes running through the systems. African leaders seek and indeed do play politics of exclusion, domineering, cultural and sectional Jingoism and even hatred thereby encouraging displacement of those who are not connected to the corridors of power. Ethno-religious attachment plays its role in displacement of citizens. For instance, the displacement that resulted from the civil unrest in Central African Republic (CAR) was caused majorly by ethno-religious inclinations. Though most of the constitutions of states parties prohibit state religion, the political actors hardly, in practice, separate religion from politics. Some political actors use religious divides to garner support from members of the respective religions thereby plunging into violence and chaos, the resultant effect of which is displacement. It is submitted that unless and until African leaders will begin to look at public office holding as service to humanity rather than personal aggrandisement, the workability of the Kampala Convention would be a mirage, at least in the near future.

The states parties are equally obliged to ensure respect for human dignity of the displaced persons; and ensure respect for the humanitarian and civilian character of protection of and assistance to internally displaced persons. The sorry state of the Internally Displaced Persons camps is one thing and the inhuman practice by those who are supposed to be care givers and protectors of the IDPs is another.

The recent report indicates that the experience of the IDPs at the various camps in the North East Nigeria is something that calls for concern. "They had been either raped in the camp or sold by those that should be protecting them in the camps". The question that readily comes to mind is, even if the convention had not been domesticated in Nigeria in line with its constitution in order to give it legal backing, is the government of Nigeria living up to its responsibility as enshrined in the same constitution regarding the welfare of its citizens? The democratically elected government of Nigeria pledged to uphold the constitution by prioritising the security and welfare of the citizens but from all indicators, it is clear that the same government has abdicated its duties. The security which the government promised and pledged to provide has not been provided, and the displaced persons who are in the various camps are not being catered for by the same government which is under obligation to so do. The security which the government promised to provide has not been seen and no arrangement is being made to improve on the existing one. Book Haram, a terrorist Islamic, group has continued to unleash terror on the innocent citizens but the government is doing little or nothing to quell it.

At the IDP camps, the government provides little or no assistance at all. The IDPs are living at the mercy of the managers of those camps. Slavery and inhumanity have become the order of the day in the camps. A recent report at the camps reveals as follows:

> *Further investigations revealed that such child trafficking business is a thriving and well-run racket in most IDP camps in the insurgency ravaged North East. It is a triangular manifestation of evil that comprises some heartless displaced persons, unscrupulous camp officials and child traffickers. Displaced persons who know the children without parents act as middlemen between the buyer and the seller. They liaise with people who come from places far flung.... The displaced person also identified the children to be sold and goes ahead to negotiate a price.... After the negotiation, the middleman approaches the camp official in charge. The official collects the money and approves the release of the kids.*

The above gives an accurate account of what transpires at the camps of the internally displaced persons (IDPs). The report further indicates that one of the reasons for the perpetration of the heinous act by the camp officials and government agents that are supposed to take care of the IDPs, is to sell other children and use the money to take care of the other children who were still in camp. Many aid workers in the IDP camps alleged that there was conspiracy of silence, which encouraged government officials in many IDP camps to continue to exploit the displaced persons. Since the officials that these cases should have been reported to were perpetrators, many victims just kept quiet for fear of being sent out of the camps.

One is not surprised at the happenings at the various IDP camps because if the government had failed to provide security for the people in their various places, the same government cannot take care of the displaced persons. If government had prevented the causes of internal displacement, the issue of slavery at the camp being perpetrated by the government officials would not have arisen. The same government cannot "ensure assistance to internally displaced persons by meeting their basic needs......" as provided for under Article 3 (1).

The convention itself does not create a binding force on the states parties but rather it gives the state parties the leverage to incorporate the obligations under the convention into their domestic legal systems. If a state party does not have the political will to incorporate the convention into its legal system, as most of them have demonstrated, the rights of the internally displaced persons are in grave jeopardy. It is submitted that since the domestic legislations seem to have had superiority over international legislations, the convention is a mere expression of the African Union's desire with little or no meaningful impact.

The other obligations contained in Articles 4, 5, 9, 10, 11, 12, 13 and 14 cannot be enforced without the obligation in Article 3(2) being fulfilled. That Article is the fulcrum or the axle around which the convention revolves. Since the states parties cannot be automatically bound by the provisions of the convention, unless the national legislatures of the various states parties will expedite action on incorporation of same into their domestic laws, the whole exercise of adoption of the Kampala Convention will be in futility. The domestication and enforcement of the convention is a collective responsibility of all members states otherwise the effect of the displacement does not affect only one member state. It has been argued that the violence in North Eastern Nigeria had caused more than 157,000 people to flee into Niger, Cameroon and Chad since the emergency rule was established some years ago. It has been posited that "the situation was becoming increasingly terrifying for refugees, locals and aid workers. UNHCR was calling for urgent humanitarian access to refugees and internally displaced people in Niger, Cameroon and Chad in order to provide much-needed emergency assistance".

The issue of terrorism or insurgency which is the principal cause of internal displacement or refugeeism should be commonly fought by the African nations. The evil of terrorism spreads like wide fire which knows no boundaries. What started like little fire known as Boko Haram insurgency in Nigeria, has been and is being spread to other neighbouring countries. Cameroon, Chad and Niger are now taking their portion of Boko Haram insurgency which was initially viewed as internal affairs of Nigeria. Good enough the Kampala convention recognises the right of African Union to intervene in the affairs of member states to prevent internal displacement. Article 8 (i) of the convention states that "The African Union shall have the right to intervene in a member state pursuant to a decision of the Assembly in accordance with Article 4(h) of the Constitutive Act in respect of grave circumstances, namely: war crimes, genocide, and crimes against humanity." The activities of the insurgents are tantamount to genocide and crimes against humanity. Many innocent citizens are killed by the various activities of insurgents and many are equally displaced. The recent steps taken by Central African Countries under the auspices of Central African Economic Community to fight Boko Haram which has recently launched onslaught against Cameroon is commendable.

It is submitted that since there are existing legal instruments such as United Nations Convention Relating to Status of Refugees, African Charter on Human and Peoples' Rights, OAU Convention Governing the Specific Aspects Convention among others, African States should cultivate the culture of domesticating and implementing them. There is need for a common confront in the fight against insurgency and other causes of internal displacement and refugeeism by the African countries. A problem that affects one part of the body, if not properly checked, will eventually affect the whole body and the consequent effect will be death. National bodies saddled with the responsibility of protecting and caring for the IDPs should live up to their duties in order to accord them their fundamental human rights. Cases of denegation, aberration and abdication of duties by the government officials should be properly investigated, if found culpable, such officials should be adequately punished in accordance with the laws of the land. Adequate arrangements should be made by the electoral bodies for the political participation of the IDPs. They are only victims of circumstances. It is only then that rights of internally displaced persons (IDPs) will be guaranteed. African Union should wake up in the area of security through its peace and security council.

CHAPTER NINE

Conflicts Management
and Resolutions

INTRODUCTION

Peace is a concept that every living being looks forward to upholding for comfortable and tranquil existence. It is a song that every nation sings even though in practice, some hardly carry it out as professed. It is in recognition of this that the human society all as a whole preaches peace among nation-states and legal instruments have been put in place from time to time for peaceful co-existence. From ages to ages, mankind has tried to prevent and manage crisis whenever it occurs. The formation of the League of Nations to prevent the outbreak of the World War II was one of the measures laid down by the global society to ensure the world peaceful co-existence. The failure of the League to prevent the occurrence of World War II resulted in its dissolution and consequently the emergence of the United Nations whose charter provides copiously for promotion of peace.

In furtherance of the peace programme of the United Nations, the Regional Organisations including Africa Union have put mechanisms to prevent or manage crisis, and maintain peace.

In May, 2004 the African Union officially launched its Peace and Security Council.[232] At the launch of the Peace and Security Council, African leaders emphasised the Council's po-

---

232   Hereinafter called the 'Council'

tential significance, claiming that its establishment "marked an historic watershed in Africa's progress towards resolving its conflicts and building of a durable peace and security order."[233]

This chapter deals with the topic in three main aspects: The historical origins, the institutional framework and evaluation or appraisal of the Council's activities from its inception to date.

HISTORICAL BACKGROUND

The Peace and Security Council was not one of the African Union's institutional organs that were originally created by the Constitutive Act of the Union, which was adopted in Lome, Togo on July 11, 2000. It rather grew out of an ad-hoc process to reform the Organisation of African Unity (OAU)[234] mechanism for conflict prevention, management and resolution, which had been adopted at the 29th ordinary session of the OAU Assembly, held in Cairo, Egypt in June 1993. The mechanism's primary objective was the anticipation and prevention of conflicts. [235]This focus on the prevention emerged after a series of debates in Dakar in 1992 and Addis Ababa in early 1993 wherein the OAU members took a conscious decision not to involve the organisation in peace-keeping operations. The member-states hoped that a focus on preventive diplomacy would be dramatically reduce the need for subsequent peace operations on the continent.[236] The consensus proved to be short-lived.

---

233   The statement of commitment to peace and security in Africa issued by the Heads of State and Government of member-states of the Peace and Security Council of African Union (AU.doc.psc/AHG/S.T(x). 25 May, 2004, par.1
234   Hereinafter called OAU
235   Williams P.D. "The Peace and Security Council of the African Union: Evaluating an embryonic International Institution" being a paper presented to the Panel "Do International Institutions have a future in International Security?" at the ISA Annual Convention, San Francisco, 26-30 March, 2005, p.3
236   Ibid.

The mass killings in Burundi and Rwanda between 1993 and 1994 in particular caused the OAU to revisit its self-imposed ban on peacekeeping. This began with series of internal debates organised by the OAU Secretariat and the circulation of a background paper summarising the issues. These discussions led to organisation's summit in 1995 in Addis Ababa, Ethiopia endorsing the idea that "ready contingents" earmarked within the African armies for deployment in peacekeeping organisations. Though there was change in principle, throughout the 1990s the OAU continued to define its priority as conflict prevention, arguing that the primary responsibility for peacekeeping in Africa lay within the United Nations.

The problem with this posture became increasingly evident as United Nations appeared to be reluctant to take the lead in conflict resolution in Africa as envisaged by OAU members. For instance, groups of West African States used ECOMOG which was a sub-regional force to resolve conflicts in Liberia, Sierra Leone and Guinea-Bissau. In 1998, factions within Southern African Development Community (SADC) did the same in response to conflicts in Lesotho and the Democratic Republic of Congo (DRC).[237] Though the arrangements received support from some members of OAU, such ad-hoc sub-regional initiatives were increasingly regarded as problematic by a vast majority of member-states and within a few years there emerged two divergent schools of thought. The first school of thought considered OAU as still being a relevant and important organisation but called for its reforms by giving it new structures and resources. The second school, however, viewed the organisation being a defunct and anachronistic institution that should

---

237   Levitt J.I "The Peace and Security Council of African Union: The Known Unknown" in Transnational Law and Contemporary Problems Journal (Spring, 2003) p.9

be closed down.[238] Most of the member-states supported this view for different reasons and it soon gained upper hand, which culminated in the decision taken at the 37th ordinary session of the Assembly in Lusaka, Tanzania in July 2001 to review the structures and working methods of OAU mechanism in the light of the establishment of a new continental organisation.[239]

The next practical step was taken when the OAU Secretary-General produced a report titled "Background Document on the Review of Structures, Procedures and Working Method of the Central Organ". This document served as the conceptual starting point for drafting of Peace and Security Council.

After mooting a range of alternative names, it was unanimously agreed at the second brainstorming retreat in South Africa in March 2002 that the new organ should be called Peace and Security Council. The first substantive proposal was for Peace and Security Council to mimic the structure of the United Nations Security Council; that it should contain five permanent and ten elected members. This position was supported by South Africa and Nigeria but rejected by the rest. The resulting position was that the Peace and Security Council would function with five members elected for terms of three years, one from each of the continent's official regions, while ten other members would be elected for terms of two years.

The meetings and discussion resorted in the adoption of the protocol which led to the establishment of Peace and Security Council of African Union in Durban, South Africa on July 9, 2002. The Council came into force on December 26, 2003 after the ratification of its protocol by 27 members out of the 53 members of the African Union. However, the Council began its work officially on March 16, 2004.

---

238   Ibid, p.100
239   P.D. Williams, op. cit.

INSTITUTIONAL FRAMEWORK OF THE COUNCIL
    By virtue of the provisions of Article 5.2 of the African Union Constitutive Act, Peace and Security Council of the Union is an organ established by the Assembly of the Union. Pursuant to the above Article, the protocol establishing the Council makes it "a standing decision-making organ for the prevention, management and resolution of conflicts."

Membership of the Peace and Security Council
    The Peace and Security Council comprises fifteen (15) members elected by Union Executive Council, that is, five elected for terms of three years and ten elected for terms of two years.
    By the provisions of Article 5 of the protocol establishing the Council, there are certain criteria to be met before a member-state will be qualified to be elected as a member of the Council. Such criteria includes stipulations that members should be chosen based on "equitable regional representation and rotation," whether such member-state had paid its dues up-to-date as well as respect for constitutional governance and the rule of law and most importantly, whether it would be able to shoulder the responsibilities that membership would place upon it.
    Apart from the fifteen elected members of the Council, interested member-states as well as other entities among others may participate in the open sessions of the Council.[240] The participation is only to the extent of the interest affecting such non-members.

---

240   Ibid p.5

The Scope and Extent of the Council

The Council's role as a standing decision-making organ for the prevention, management and resolution of conflicts is expected to be a collective security and early-warning arrangement to facilitate timely and efficient response to conflict and crisis situations in Africa.[241]

It has been argued that instead of being proactive, the Council has devoted relatively little attention to the prevention of conflict, or addressing structural issues that encourage bad governance.[242] The Council has forgotten that its role is three-way thronged. It has to first of all prevent the occurrence of eruption of crisis in member-states using the available tools like AU Troops and other logistics to prevent eruption of crisis where there are threats of same. Even if the Council cannot prevent or nip crisis in the bud, the management of the crisis seems to be better imagined than experienced. The last aspect of the role which is resolution of crisis seems to be the only focus of the Commission.

The Council's different types of operations are set out in six different scenarios envisaged for the African Standby Force (ASF).[243] In all the scenarios, actions are required to be taken in 30 days except scenario six wherein actions are required to be taken within 14 days of the eruption of such crisis.

However, a crisis has been detected between the Council and UN Security Council in the area of which the body has the primary legal authority to sanction the use of military force in crisis-prone areas. Articles 16 and 17 of the Peace and Security

---

241   See Article 2.1 of the PSC Protocol; see also Protocol to the Constitutive Act, which amended Article 5 of the Act to make PSC an organ of the Union in 2003.

242   P.D. Williams op. cit.

243   See the Roadmap for the operationalization of the African Standby Force (AU doc. EXP/AU-RECS/ASF/4(I) Addis Ababa, 22-23 March, 2005) Para A-1

Council's protocol appear to contradict each other. Article 16.1 states that the primary responsibility for promoting peace, security and stability in Africa belonged to African Union whereas Article 17.1 provides acknowledged that the UN Security Council has the primary responsibility for the maintenance of international peace and security. If the same protocol recognizes the primary responsibility of United Nations' Security Council to maintain peace and security internationally, it is submitted that the best approach is to adopt the doctrine of covering the field. The courts in Nigeria have provided an answer to the issue herein. In **A-G Abia State v. A-G Federation (2002) FWLR (Pt.101) 1419** the Supreme Court held that where both the State House of Assembly and the National Assembly have concurrent jurisdiction to legislate on a subject matter and there is a conflict between both legislations, the Act of the National Assembly shall be interpreted to have covered the field on the subject matter.

It is submitted that since the UN Security Council is a world body with similar responsibility of maintaining peace and security in the world, (including Africa wherein Peace and Security Council of African Union operates) it has the primary responsibility of sanctioning military force in times of conflict or crisis.

While reacting to this situation, the then legal adviser to African Union, Kioko, in his opinion stated as follows:

> In deciding an intervention, the African Union will have to consider whether it will seek authorization of the UN Security Council as it is required to do under Article 53 of the UN Charter. When questions were raised as to whether the Union could possibly have an inherent right to intervene other than through the Security Council, they were dismissed out of hand. This decision reflected

a sense of frustration with the slow pace of reform of the international order, and with instances in which the international community tended to focus attention on other parts of the world at the expense of more pressing problems in Africa.[244]

What however, appears to be a succor to the AU Peace and Security Council is that the UN Security Council seems not to be bothered about the usurpation of its powers by regional or sub-regional organisations. Article 53 of the United Nations Charter allows the regional or sub-regional organisation to seek its authorisation before deciding to intervene in such crisis situation. This provision of the charter has however, been sometimes kept aside by regional or sub-regional bodies with a view to bringing peace within their domains. For instance, when the Economic Community of West African States (ECOWAS) organized peacekeeping forces under the auspices of ECOMOG for Sierra Leone and Liberia, it took the decision and went into action without the authorisation from United Nations until sometime later. Similarly, the Eastern African Region imposed trade and economic sanctions in 1996 without resort to the United Nations but the action was endorsed by the then Organisation of African Unity (OAU). Far from Africa, the North Atlantic Treaty Organisation (NATO) intervened in Kosovo in 1999 without the authorization of the United Nations. Though this action was condemned by United States as being illegal, the NATO action found its backing in the Genocide Convention of 1948. The in-

---

244   B. Kioki, 'The right of intervention under the African Union Constitutive Act: From non-interference to non-intervention; International Review of the Red Cross, 2003 85:852 p.821

tervention by NATO was to put to an end continued genocide in that country. [245]

For the purpose of clarity, Article 53 of the United Nations Charter provides that:

> The Security Council shall where appropriate, utilise such regional arrangements or agencies for enforcement action under its authority. But no enforcement action shall be taken under regional arrangements or by regional agencies without the authorization of the Security Council.

As clear as the provisions of the above article appear to be the United Nations seems to be looking at the intent rather than the form. Be that as it may, the inaction of the United Nations even when its power and authority have been usurped by regional arrangements might be considered to be in the interest of world peace. If UN could insist on its rights in such situations, its aims and objectives may be defeated; all that is needed is almost peace and security of the world. Where the regional arrangements are capable of maintaining peace without the intervention of the World Body, it will lessen the work for the UN provided the ultimate goal of peace is achieved.

Some commentators have posited that the Protocol relating to the establishment of peace and security has stipulated that the Peace and Security Council shall cooperate with the United Nations Security Council, which has the primary responsibility for the maintenance of international peace and se-

---

245   T. Maluwa, "Reimaging African Unity: Some preliminary reflections on the Constitutive Act of the African Union (2002)" African Yearbook of International Law (Vol.9 2001) pp.7-8; See also C. Portella, Humanitarian Intervention, NATO and International Law: Can the Institution of Humanitarian Intervention Justify unauthorized action?" p.3

curity, and that, where necessary, recourse shall be had to the United Nations to provide the necessary financial, logistical and military support.[246]

Procedural Operations of Peace and Security

In order to achieve its set goals, the Council has, through the protocol establishing it, laid down some procedural rules. By virtue of Article 8.12 of the protocol, each member of the Council is entitled to one vote. But before the voting right could be exercised by members, the general principal of consensus would be adopted first.[247] Where the consensus option fails, then the Council shall make its decisions on procedural matters by a simple majority while decisions on all other matters shall be made by a two-thirds majority of members voting. It has been contended that the use of consensus approach by the Council since its inception has made it to be "understood as a social environment within which the micro-processes of the socialization (persuasion and social influence) operate both among the Peace and Security Council members and between the wider group of the AU member states and the AU Commission. [248]

The Council meets a minimum of two times per month at the ambassadorial level, one time per month at ministerial level, while at Heads of State level it meets once in a year. The agenda for a meeting is usually determined in the light of ongoing crisis and conflict situations, proposal from a Council member or via a proposal from the Commission for Peace and Security. The Council holds three different types of meetings, namely: formal meetings wherein the reports from AU Commission are examined and reacted upon. Secondly, the Commission also holds

---

246   B. Kioki op. cit. p.822
247   See Article 8.13
248   P.D Williams op. cit. p.8

briefing sessions. At these meetings, (briefing sessions), staff of the Council update it on specific issues rather than full reports. After hearing the talking points, members of the Council decide whether to make a mere statement or to issue a communiqué, depending on the magnitude of the matter. Thirdly, consultation meetings are held, certain actors in crisis situations are invited for informal consultations.

Norms

In line with the provisions in the AU Constitutive Act, United Nations Charter and Universal Human Rights Declaration, the Council sets out its guiding principles.[249] Principles (j) and (k) recognize the African Union's right of intervention in respect of what is called grave areas or circumstances such as war crimes, genocide and crime against humanity as provided in Article 4(h) of the Constitutive Act. Whatever however remains doubtful is the implementation of the provisions of both the Constitutive Act and the protocol establishing the Council.

The Council's Mandate

As the name of the Council implies, its mandate is to promote peace and security of the African continent as provided in Article 3(f) of the Constitutive Act of the African Union.[250] The Council's protocol has outlined six objectives for its operation.[251] These include (1) promotion of peace, security and stability in Africa; (2) to anticipate and prevent conflicts; (3) to promote and implement peace-building and post conflict reconstruction activities; (4) to coordinate and harmonise continental efforts in

---

249   See Article 4 of PSC Protocol
250   The Article which deals with the objectives provides that the objectives of the Union shall be to (f) "promote peace, security and stability on the Continent."
251   See Article 3 of the Protocol

the prevention of international terrorism in all its aspects; (5) to develop a common defence policy for the Union; and (6) to encourage democratic practices, good governance and the rule of law as well as protect human rights and fundamental freedoms. The Council is to be supported by other instruments of the Union to achieve its set goals.

HOW HAS THE COUNCIL PERFORMED SINCE ITS INCEPTION?

Security and peace of every community, nation/state or continent is paramount and very germane to its growth. Without peace, there will be no progress. A society without peace is always in pieces. It is in realization of this indispensable truth that the African Union set up the Peace and Security Council to prevent occurrence of violent conflict among member states; and where conflicts had already erupted, the Council should manage same with a view to resolving it.[252]

The protocol relating to the establishment of the Council has mandated it to perform the functions of peace support operations and intervention among others as provided under Article 4(h) and (j) of the African Union's Constitutive Act.[253] By this, the Council is to intervene in member nations with the aid of African Standby Force, composed of multi-disciplinary contingents, with civilian and military components, to carry out peace support operations.[254] The Force is to operate at three possible levels: as an African Force under African Union (Continental Force); as Regional Brigade at the level of Regional mechanism for conflict prevention, management and resolution, or at the

---

252   See Article 3(f) of the Constitutive Act
253   See Articles 6 and 7 of the Protocol
254   See Article 4(h) and (j) of the AU Constitutive Act

level of lead nation intervening on behalf of the African Union.[255] The question that is yet to be answered is, has the Council been utilizing these instrumentalities to achieve its set goals? This certainly will be greeted with mixed answers.

The greatest monster facing the Council with challenge to the Council is terrorism/insurgency. This monster has ravaged almost half of the continent, yet the effect of the Council is felt little or not at all. Insurgency or terrorism has pervaded all the regions of the continent. Countries such as Central African Republic, Nigeria, Somalia, Libya, to mention but a few, have been ravaged or annihilated by the terrorist groups such as Boko Haram, Al-Shabab, etc.

In Somalia, the terrorists have taken three-quarters of the country wherein they hoisted their flags claiming superiority and control over these areas.[256] Nigeria, the "giant of Africa" has had her fair share of terrorism. Boko Haram terrorists have persistently claimed to have taken over some towns like Goza, Damboa, Biu, Barma, inter alia, thereby hoisting their flags and proclaiming these areas Islamic state. Insurgency has engulfed States like Benue, Borno, Adamawa, Plateau, Taraba, Yobe among others. In Libya, Bengazi and Tripoli, the nation's capital city, are under terrorist siege.[257] Recently, the Nigerian National Assembly through its leadership (the Speaker of the House of Representatives and the President of the Senate) decried that some Local Government Areas had been taken over by the insurgents.[258] In the face of all this, the Peace and Security Council seems to be adamant. No proactive or positive reaction steps

---

255 See B. Kioki op. cit. p.824
256   See Daily Trust Newspaper of 31st July, 2014, p.51
257   See Daily Trust Newspaper of August 1, 2014, p.31
258   They made the assertions on 16/9/2014 when they resumed from the two months annual recess.

are taken to prevent and or manage the situations with a view to resolving them.

Some commentators have outlined some factors militating against the smooth operations of the Council.[259] The first challenge is funding/finance. It has been argued that the cost of interventions by the Council in conflict- inflicted countries, will no doubt be quite high, and the African Union, not being a very well-endowed organisation financially, will find that it will of necessity have to involve the international community at large, and the United Nations Security Council, which has the primary responsibility of maintaining international peace, for it to succeed.[260] This school of thought places reliance on the situations in Liberia and Sierra Leone wherein Nigeria, the "giant of Africa" singlehandedly bore the responsibility of sponsoring the peacekeeping forces.

The second problem identified by the school of thought is incompatible equipment, which makes it difficult for the peacekeeping force to contend with the insurgents. The third issue identified is political or other factors. For one, there may be lack of political will by the strong nations to intervene in conflict situations as well as the battle of supremacy by those nations. The case of Nigeria is a classic example. Since Boko Haram insurgency started in Nigeria, most of the neighbouring countries remain aloof to it. The recent seizure of $15 million (USD) belonging to Nigerian government, which was allegedly meant for the purchase of 'arms' to fight terrorism in the country, by the South African authorities, clearly shows that the member-states are not willing and ready to cooperate for the fight against terrorism. If South Africa which is one of the "super powers" on the continent would engage in the cold war with another African

---

259   B. Kioki op. cit. p.822
260   Ibid

"giant," Nigeria, certainly the battle against the common enemy will suffer a setback. It is submitted that for the Council and by extension the continent to succeed in its fight against insurgency and terrorism, which are the major sources of conflict in Africa, there must be political will among the member-states, particularly the big brothers.

When the terrorists launched their onslaught against Nigeria, the neighbouring countries felt reluctant to unite with Nigeria in the fight against terrorism. Howbeit, recently, the wife of the Deputy Prime Minister of Cameroon was abducted by the same Boko Haram terrorists who attacked some towns in Cameroon. Also, when Libya was being ravaged by terrorists, other African countries felt that it was internal problem of that country. However, the repercussions and or aftermaths of the conflict are being felt by the other countries on the continent. Even the effects of the crisis in the Central African Republic had been inhaled by other countries in Africa.

Another school of thought with its proponents such as Irobi, Doyle, Gough, Ikejiaku among others have looked at conflict resolution in Africa in a different perspective. They argue that developed and underdeveloped economies should strive to meet their citizens' needs and that these needs are not really the same in both types of economies. In Africa, strategies such as coercive methods as implied by the power politics, balance of power, and use of state agents to suppress conflicts, would be ineffective in modifying the conflict behaviours, resolution of conflicts and con-sequent creating peace in the continent if/ when the basis of the conflict is unmet human basic needs. In other words, conflict resolution should not still mean the use of adequate force to bring about some desired result. However, if social conditions were the problem, then conflict resolution and prevention would be possible and effective by removing the sources of conflict: institutions could adjust social norms to the needs of persons. For example, there should be improvement in the nature and mode of governance in Africa to accommodate and benefit the masses, that is, the poor. This may involve stimulated thinking that considers all shades of opinion or that brings together different points of view. There are acceptable means for example, of giving a sense of identity to the person at the workplace, to young people, to minorities and ethnic groups, and catering to the need to provide food, water, housing, electricity, health, education, and other necessities of life. There is the need to consider these basic human needs in Africa as a strategy of preventing conflicts. Unlike the above theory (and other theories), which point to inherent aggressiveness as the source of conflicts, the basic human needs theory grounds political violence and social instability in unmet basic human needs (as a result of allure in government), and it focuses on peaceful resolution of conflicts. This will be the framework for analysing conflict and conflict resolution in this perspective. This perspective, therefore, will employ the human basic needs theory for understanding conflict and its resolution in Africa, particularly in the cases of Zimbabwean (2008) and Kenyan (2007) conflicts and the efforts to achieve a peaceful resolution. That is to say, conflict resolution means getting to the roots or remote cause of the problems and resolving them in ways that further the longer-term goals of all concerned the human needs theory deals with these.

The 2008 election conducted in Zimbabwe was the immediate event that directed to the conflict, thereby deepening the political and social crisis in the country. President Mugabe 28 years in the mantle of leadership then had been characterized by bad policies, corruption, and repressive governance and his ZANU-PF party bears primary responsibility for the severe economic slide, growing public discontent, and Zimbabwe's international isolation. Zimbabwe, in March 29, 2008, held joint presidential and parliamentary elections that were blemished by a high level of pre-poll manipulation. The elections were officially witnessed or observed by only countries, institutions, and other representatives that were seen as very friendly and other neutral bodies and institutions, mostly Western media, were barred from observing the elections. Though the election activities were distorted, amidst manipulations by the ZANU-PF, the citizens of Zimbabwe clearly indicated or rather demonstrated their rejection of the status quo that was the then current political situation in Zimbabwe. This is because for the first time, ZANU-PF lost control of parliament to the opposition party, the Movement for Democratic Change (MDC), which made extraordinary and unmatched gains in rural areas. The African Briefing No. 51 of May 21, 2008 described the scenario in its report: The 29 March 2008 elections have dramatically changed Zimbabwe's political landscape.

For the first time since independence in 1980, Robert Mugabe ran second in the presidential voting, and the opposition the Movement for Democratic Change (MDC) won control of parliament. The MDC went to the polls deeply divided, but Morgan Tsvangirai and his party regained their authority by winning despite an uneven playing field. However, rather than allowing the spirit of democratic tenets to reign or take its course, the ruling party under Robert Mugabe and his radical supporters took all possible steps to thwart the genuine outcome of the elections and thereby coerce victory. For example, they took uncompromising moves, such as withholding the results of the presidential election, launching a country-wide campaign of violence, repression, and intimidation. This bad political climate and political posture of the ruling party under Mugabe forced

Tsvangirai the opposition leader to withdraw from the second round run-off of the presidential election fixed on June 27, 2008, over election hostilities. Due to the increase of domestic, regional, and international condemnation and criticism regarding the non free and unfair election and violence, the ZANU-PF and the two MDC divisions began initiating talks on July 24, under the mediation of South African President Mbeki. The series of peace talks and negotiations finally culminated in a power-sharing deal between Mugabe and Tsvangirai that was eventually signed on September 11, 2008. The implementation of this power-sharing deal, however, has seriously been impeded, since the ruling party under Mugabe refused to put this deal into effect.

Within this period, the general welfare and humanitarian situation for the majority of Zimbabweans had continued to deteriorate. There had been food shortages; inadequate health care services and other necessary social facilities for the citizens, causing the outbreak of diseases, such as a cholera epidemic; and inflation became so high that the cost of basic necessities became out of the reach of an average Zimbabwean. For example, according to the Confederation of Zimbabwe Industry (CZI), industrial output was at about one-third of its pre-2000 level, resulting in a negative economic growth rate of À4: 4%. Recent data from the Consumer Council of Zimbabwe (CCZ) puts annual inflation above 13,000%, rate the International Monetary Fund (IMF) predicted could reach 100,000% by the end of that year. Four out of five Zimbabweans were unemployed, basic commodities such as bread, sugar, and maize meal were unobtainable, and shortages of fuel, electricity, and water were a daily occurrence; social services had broken down, with hospitals and clinics operating without adequate medical equipment or supplies. Also the African Group pictured and reported the scenario thus: Zimbabweans continue to face economic turmoil and corruption, severe food shortages and the collapse of vital services. HIV/ AIDS among adults stand at over 20%, while a mounting cholera epidemic has left over 1,500 dead. By January 2009 the annual inflation rate stood at over 200%, the world's highest by far making day-to-day life for Zimbabwe increasingly difficult. Up to a third of the population is thought to have fled over recent years, and remittances from the growing Diasporas have become a lifeline for many remaining. The human needs theory emphasizes the problems of the (domestic) institution of government unable to meet the basic needs of the population as the source of conflicts. As argued, Burton points out that aggressions and conflicts are the direct result of some institutions and social norms being incompatible with human needs. He tends to emphasize the failure of existing state systems to satisfy any of these needs, which is the primary source of modern ethno-nationalist struggles.

In Zimbabwe, the denial or neglect of the basic needs (e.g., material needs and neglect of certain identities, such as the human cost of unemployment to the youths and land rights) by the government of Mugabe is the remote source of the conflict. Just as the theory stipulates, when such nonnegotiable basic needs are not met, conflict is inevitable. In response to the conflict in Zimbabwe, there has been a chorus of condemnation from Western leaders and the international community, such as the United Nations Security Council, European Union, and African regional organization and civil society, such as the African Union (AU) and South African Development Community (SADC) over the withholding of the results and the rising violence.

The Kenyan crisis of 2007/2008, which comes in the form of political, economic, and humanitarian crises, was the direct consequence of the December 27, 2007 presidential election.

The crisis erupted after the incumbent President Mwai Kibaki was declared the winner. However, Raila Odinga of the Orange Democratic Movement (ODM) and his supporters alleged electoral malpractice; this allegation was widely confirmed by both domestic and international observers. The announcement and swearing-in of Kibaki was followed by a mix of opposing reactions from the supporters of ODM coalition because of their ethnic and geographical diversity. Besides staging of nonviolent protests, opposition supporters engaged in violent rampages in different parts of the country, most noticeable in Odinga's home of Nyanza Province, the slums of Nairobi, and part of his Langata constituency. The crisis that was more of targeted ethnic violence rather than violent protests intensified and was initially directed against the people of Kikuyu, the community in which Kibaki is a member. This particularly affected those living outside their traditional settlement areas, mainly in the Rift-Valley Province.

The violence intensified when over 30 unarmed civilians were killed in a church near Eldoret on New Year's Day (the Rift-Valley has been known for tensions, which caused a lot of violence in past elections in Kenya). Some of the people in Kikuyu were also involved in violence against the opposition groups that supported Odinga, especially Luos and Kalenjin and basically in the areas surrounding Nakuru and Naivasha. In Mombasa, Kenyan Muslims took to the street to protest the electoral manipulations and air their own grievances. Though ethnic tension played a role in these protests, hardship being experienced by the masses, especially the poor actually intensified the violence, as looters also struck a number of stores in Mombasa. The slums of Nairobi saw some of the worst violence, some were ethnically motivated attacks, some acts of outrage at extreme poverty, and some the activities of criminal gangs. The violence continued sporadically for several months, particularly in the Rift Valley. It is important to point out that it was also clear that the long-standing conflicts over land, social injustice, especially deepening poverty and inequality fuelled the crisis. According to different estimates at least 1,000, but perhaps more than 1,500 people were killed altogether, mainly in the Rift-Valley, Nyanza province, and Nairobi. At least 3,500 people (but probably a much higher number) were evicted from their homes, mostly in the Rift-Valley.

As argued, according to the human needs theory, conflict is likely to occur when the institution of governance neglects or fails to meet the basic needs of its citizens (e.g., basic material needs, needs of identity, recognition needs, needs of security and protection needs of self fulfilment). The importance of these basic needs differ from the South and the North, developed and developing world, rich and poor countries.

However in Africa, the most important need for now is that of basic material needs, such as food, water, health, shelter, good roads and basic education. The fact is that most governments in Africa have failed the people in providing their basic needs, and this is the remote or primary cause of most of the conflicts in the continent. When the masses notice that the government they elected into power cannot deliver, in the form of meeting their basic needs, they normally vote such governments out of power in the subsequent election. However, the fact is that once elected into power, most leaders are very reluctant or unwilling to step down from the corridors of power; hence the consequential conflict(s).In relation to Kenya's case, the main stake in this most recent election was whether voters would re-elect Kibaki, who had brought great expectations to the 2002 election. However during his term in office, there was disillusionment over his aspirations to new politics, and particularly, the lack of improvement of social and economic conditions of the majority, and morally unjust political life, especially due to a consistently high level of corruption and worsening inequalities as the country experienced rapid economic growth. With inequalities which were already high at the beginning of Kibaki's term (the country was ranked tenth on the world's list of countries with the highest level of inequality in terms of wealth),worsening and the HDI continuing to drop since 1990. It is true that when a poorly performing economy begins to grow quickly, as was the case in Kenya, the inequalities become more pronounced. The growth which was concentrated on the service industry only benefited part of the population, which was close to the president. While the poorest classes experienced reduction in their purchasing power. Kenyan youth, who make up the majority of the population, felt particularly neglected. In a country where life expectancy is 55 years, the persistent under-employment in this section of the population can only be troubling. As early as during the 2005 constitutional referendum, which the opposition-backed, no campaign won, voters had opted to punish the disappointing government personified by an ageing and a stuttering president.

It is reasonable to argue that because the Kibaki government was not able to deliver the wishes of the people, essentially by providing their basic needs, he was voted out in the December election in 2007 (this was the view of most domestic and international observers during the election in Kenya). The officially-declared victory of the presidential election by the incumbent President Mwai Kibaki was disputed by the opposition, civil society, domestic and international observers alike. In a rather surprising move the international community stood united, did not endorse the presidential election results and put pressure on Kenya's political leaders to solve the crisis. The initial reluctance by the ruling party to heed the call of the people (both domestic and international) was followed by the post-election crisis, amidst violence and hostility. Analysts describe the scenario during the violence thus: The arson of the church at Eldoret at New Year's Day, with at least 35 refugees inside being burnt alive, constituted perhaps the most gruesome example of violence in Kenya's post election crisis. Attacks on settlers in the Rift Valley probably left several hundred of people dead; the fear they generated accounted for the vast majority of the casualties. About 300,000 people were initially displaced during the first two weeks of the crisis. Therefore, it is believed that the best conflict resolution strategy in Kenya and supposedly, in most conflict-ridden African states, would be to concentrate on the improvement of the institution of governance, in relation to its inability to fulfil the basic needs of the people, as Burton's human needs theory stipulates.

The African Union was established in order to respond to the problem of conflicts in the African continent. When African leaders adopted the AU Act in 2000, they were crucially conscious of the fact that the scourge of conflicts in Africa constitutes a major impediment to the socio economic development of the continent and of the need to promote peace, security, and stability as a prerequisite for the implementation of a development and integration agenda. Consequently, the Act sets out as some of its objectives, promotion of peace and security, and stability on the continent, and establishment of the necessary conditions that enable the continent to play its rightful role in the global economy and in international negotiations. These objectives are supported by principles including the establishment of a common defence policy for the African continent; the peaceful resolution of conflicts among member states of the union through such appropriate means as may be decided upon by the Assembly and; the prohibition of the use of force or threat to use force among others.

The performance of the Peace and Security Council is greatly influenced by the political will of the member states who are the members of the General Assembly wherein the decision to intervene is taken. That being the case, the Union finds it difficult to take drastic measures in dealing with the leaders who predominantly make up the General Assembly. The Peaceful Resolution of conflict mechanism of the Union does not yield result either. Since the powerful leaders of the member states who perpetrate the heinous acts are the ones who partake in the decision making of the General Assembly, it renders the union handicapped in resolving conflict in Africa. The recent political crises in Burundi and Guinea Bissau do not speak well about the union and its conflict resolution approach. It is submitted that the union needs to strengthen its conflict resolution mechanism in order to achieve the desired results.

CHAPTER TEN

The Way Forward

The primary motive of writing this book is to assess African Union's performance in the past one decade with a view to discovering to what extent it has achieved basic objectives of establishing it. Readers and scholars are interested in The Constitutive Act of the African Union with its laudable and robust achievable objectives, which if fully implemented, will put Africa on the path of development. However, it appeared that African leaders are more interested in goal setting than goal actualisation especially their formation and management of African Union. Providing direction is more than just issuing directives, says Ann Phillips, a senior consulting partner with Ken Blanchard Companies. In the same vein, providing leadership is more difficult than mere setting up of institutions like the case of African Union. From the days of Organisation of African Union (OAU) to the present African Union, African leaders have failed to demonstrate sufficient political will in dealing with critical issues that seems to challenge the continent that led to the formation of African Union. In the words of Phillips, Leaders often believe they are providing direction when they tell people to 'Do this, and then do that, and be sure to get it done by this date,' but that is only part of providing direction—and probably the lowest form of the behaviour.

African leaders have to get started in their attempt to join the rest of the world by doing what leaders do and produce result. Application of political will remain the first foundation by any leader. What is political will in the first place? Political will" refers to the fact that when passing any law there may be some political cost as the law may upset some people and please others. "Political will" refers to that collective amount of political benefits and costs that would result from the passage of any given law.

Xenophobia attacks between the months of March and April 2015 serve as an outstanding example of leadership failure in the African Continent. Why on earth should generation of people that suffered various forms of deprivations in the hands of white minorities in the days of Apartheid regime continue to visit similar treatments on fellow Africans? It will be recalled that the xenophobic practice came into full force when democratic government came on board in South Africa in 1994. The ANC government – in its attempts to overcome the divides of the past and build new forms of social cohesion... embarked on an aggressive and inclusive nation-building project. One unanticipated by-product of this project has been a growth in intolerance towards outsiders... Violence against foreign citizens and African refugees has become increasingly common and communities are divided by hostility and suspicion.

The study on a citizen survey across member states of the Southern African Development Community (SADC) carried out a research and found South Africans expressing the harshest anti-foreigner sentiment, with 21% of South Africans in favour of a complete ban on entry by foreigners and 64% in favour of strict limitations on the numbers allowed. By contrast, the next-highest proportion of respondents in favour of a total ban on foreigners was in neighbouring Namibia and Botswana, at 10%.

Foreigners and the South African Police Service

A 2004 study by the Centre for the Study of Violence and Reconciliation (CSVR) of attitudes among police officers in the Johannesburg area found that 87% of respondents believed that most undocumented immigrants in Johannesburg are involved in crime, despite there being no statistical evidence to substantiate the perception. Such views combined with the vulnerability of illegal aliens led to abuse, including violence and extortion, some analysts argued.

In a March 2007 meeting with home affairs minister Nosiviwe Mapisa-Nqakula a representative of Burundian refugees in Durban claimed immigrants could not rely on police for protection but instead found police mistreating them, stealing from them and making unfounded allegations that they sell drugs. Two years earlier, at a similar meeting in Johannesburg, Mapisa-Nqakula had admitted that refugees and asylum seekers were mistreated by police with xenophobic attitudes.

Violence before May 2008

According to a 1998 Human Rights Watch report immigrants from Malawi, Zimbabwe and Mozambique living in the Alexandra township were "physically assaulted over a period of several weeks in January 1995, as armed gangs identified suspected undocumented migrants and marched them to the police station in an attempt to 'clean' the township of foreigners. The campaign, known as "Buyelekhaya" (go back home), blamed foreigners for crime, unemployment and sexual attacks.

In September 1998 a Mozambican and two Senegalese were thrown out of a train. The assault was carried out by a group returning from a rally that blamed foreigners for unemployment, crime and spreading AIDS.

In 2000 seven foreigners were killed on the Cape Flats over a five-week period in what police described as xenophobic murders possibly motivated by the fear that outsiders would claim property belonging to locals.

In October 2001 residents of the Zandspruit informal settlement gave Zimbabweans 10 days to leave the area. When the foreigners failed to leave voluntarily they were forcefully evicted and their shacks were burned down and looted. Community members said they were angry that Zimbabweans were employed while locals remained jobless and blamed the foreigners for a number of crimes. No injuries were reported among the Zimbabweans.

In the last week of 2005 and first week of 2006 at least four people, including two Zimbabweans, died in the Olievenhoutbosch settlement after foreigners were blamed for the death of a local man. Shacks belonging to foreigners were set alight and locals demanded that police remove all immigrants from the area.

In August 2006 Somali refugees appealed for protection after 21 Somali traders were killed in July of that year and 26 more in August. The immigrants believed the murders to be motivated by xenophobia, although police rejected the assertion of a concerted campaign to drive Somali traders out of townships in the Western Cape.

Attacks on foreign nationals increased markedly in late 2007 and it is believed that there were at least a dozen attacks between January and May 2008. The most severe incidents occurred on 8 January 2008 when two Somali shop owners were murdered in the Eastern Cape towns of Jeffreys Bay and East London and in March 2008 when seven people were killed including Zimbabweans, Pakistanis and a Somali after their shops and shacks were set alight in Atteridgeville near Pretoria.

Spread of Violence

On 12 May 2008 a series of riots started in the township of Alexandra (in the north-eastern part of Johannesburg) when locals attacked migrants from Mozambique, Malawi and Zimbabwe, killing two people and injuring 40 others. Some attackers were reported to have been singing Jacob Zuma's campaign song Umshini Wami (Zulu: "Bring Me My Machine Gun").

In the following weeks the violence spread, first to other settlements in the Gauteng Province, then to the coastal cities of Durban and Cape Town.

Attacks were also reported in parts of the Southern Cape, Mpumalanga, the North West and Free State.

Popular Opposition to Xenophobia

In Khutsong in Gauteng and the various shack settlements governed by Abahlali base Mjondolo in KwaZulu-Natal social movements were able to ensure that there were no violent attacks. The Western Cape Anti-Eviction Campaign also organised against xenophobia. Pallo Jordan argues that "Active grassroots interventions contained the last wave of xenophobia"

Therefore, the recent wave of attack shouldn't have come to the member states of African Union. The above precedence would have been enough for the regional body to take a decisive step as to how to halt the ugly development in the continent. One may wish to ask if what is happening in South Africa can ever happen within the European Union member states. The Union has only succeeded in putting in place legal framework that they have refused to implement.

Readers should examine the following fourteen points objectives and analyse the extent of success by the African Union thus; achieving greater unity and solidarity between the African countries and Africans, defending the sovereignty, territorial integrity and independence of its Member States, accelerating the political and social-economic integration of the continent, promoting and defending African common positions on issues of interest to the continent and its peoples, encourage international cooperation, taking due account of the Charter of the United Nations and the Universal Declaration of Human Rights, promoting peace, security, and stability on the continent, promoting democratic principles and institutions, popular participation and good governance, promote and protect human and peoples' rights in accordance with the African Charter on Human and Peoples' Rights and other relevant human rights instruments, establishing the necessary conditions which enable the continent to play its rightful role in the global economy and in international negotiations, promote sustainable development at the economic, social and cultural levels as well as the integration of African economies, promote co-operation in all fields of human activity to raise the living standards of African peoples, coordinate and harmonise the policies between the existing and future Regional Economic Communities for the gradual attainment of the objectives of the Union, advance the development of the continent by promoting research in all fields, in particular in science and technology, work with relevant international partners in the eradication of preventable diseases and the promotion of good health on the continent.

Taking a cue from the above, there is no denying the fact that the various leaders in the continent have put in place a very beautify road map if only there will be a political will that will produce the actionable steps of realizing the objectives. if

219

the road map as being laid out is seriously implemented and harnessed, it will bring the much desired development in Africa.

However, the need to adhere to the provisions of the Constitutive Act of the African Union and other legal instruments cannot be overemphasised. The development of the continent should not be attached or attributed to the mere creation of institutional structures in form of regional organisations. It goes far beyond that. The creation of those institutional structures will only bring impact when they perform to the expectations of the masses. Peace and security of the continent must be a priority at any given time. The political instability in many African countries portrays African Union as being least emancipatory. The lulation that is currently greeting the Union's activities is quite unfortunate. There is need for reverse in trend of the Union's workings. Any issue affecting the continent negatively should not be treated with kid gloves by the Union. African Union should rise up to the present day realities and put the continent on the right track. The dream of the founding fathers should be kept alive by the current crop of African leaders and those to come. African Union should serve as a medium through which the continent could speak and the whole world would respect. This could only be done when the Union takes decisions and stand by them by implementing them without delay. The African political leaders who are the custodian of the Union must be seen to be walking their talk.

What should be done?

There is general consensus that a lot of work has to be done by the Union for the betterment of Africa, therefore, it is apposite to proffer some suggestions or recommendations that will help the African Union achieve its set goals. The current pace of implementation of the Union's Charters is to slow and non purposeful to achieve the desired goals as enunciated above.

As a recommendation from my own point of view, first, for better performance and consequent achievement of the African Union's set goals, the Assembly of the Union, which is regarded as the supreme Organ should be proactive instead of reactive to the challenges facing the Union. Whatever decision taken by the Assembly either at its sessions or through the reports of other organs, it should be taken seriously with a view to implementing it. This will prevent certain foreseeable calamities that have befallen the continent in the recent past. Again, if the Assembly takes any decision, it should be implemented without fear or favour. Being dicey after having taken decision will exacerbate the situation.

Second, other organs of the Union which are subject to the Assembly of the Union such as executive Council, Pan-African Parliament, should be made independent in order to ensure their maximum performance. The current position where their performance is subject to the assignment of duties by the Assembly inhibits their maximum performance. Since their performance is subject to the overall performance of the Assembly, its failure will automatically affect the other organs that are subject to it and this will not be in the interest of the continent.

Third, human rights are inalienable; therefore, they should be given the needed maximum attention. The situation whereby human and peoples' rights are trampled upon without an eye-brow from the Union is quite alarming. The ineptitude of the African Union and its negligent attitude has sent many African citizens to their early graves. Human lives are cheaply taken away by the few opportunistic leaders without any reaction from the Union. For instance, thousands of innocent lives are being destroyed in Cote d'Ivoire and Libya but African Union in its characteristic attitude has remained adamant, even though the Union's Constitutive Act forbids it. This therefore, calls for intensification of efforts by the Union in the area of promotion and protection of human and peoples' rights in order to achieve one of its objectives. Again, in order to ensure maximum protection of human rights, the protocol on the Statute for African Court of Justice and Human Rights should be amended to allow private individuals and Non-Governmental Organisations (NGOs) direct access to the court to seek redress any time they allege that their rights have been, are being or likely to be violated. This is the only way that African Court of Justice and Human Rights will be regarded as the hope of the common man.

Fourth, African Charter on Democracy, Elections and Governance adopted in 2007 should be implemented to the letter in order to entrench democratisation in Africa. If the charter is followed to the letter, those leaders such as Laurent Gbagbo, Robert Mugabe, Muammar Gadhafi among others who cling unto power against the will of the people will have nowhere to hide again. This is because in international law, once a state enters into an agreement by way of signing a treaty, it is bound by it, and cannot derogate from its provisions. Since the charter prevents or prohibits unconstitutional change of government including refusal to handover power by an incumbent after losing election, if fully implemented, such leaders will be ousted by use of reasonable force. Similar legal instruments are being used by the Organization of American States (OAS) and European Community and they are helping them.

Fifth, New Partnership for African Development (NEPAD) which is the programme for the implementation of the Union's developmental agenda should be strengthened by contributing financially to its activities. Its funding should be made compulsory by all member states. The present position where funding has been made voluntary by member states is not in the interest of the continent, most member states have not been contributing to the partnership thereby thwarting its activities. Moreover, member states should submit their developmental programmes and projects to African Peer Review Mechanism (APRM) which is the engine through which the partnership performs for assessment and recommendations.

Sixth, the financial institutions of the Union should be put in motion so as to grease the engine of Africa's development. When such institutions like African Central Bank, African Monetary Fund and African Investment Bank have become operational, the economic activities as well as cooperation will be easier. The steering committee for the establishment of African Central Bank currently sitting in Abuja should expedite actions in order to bring it to fruition. Central Bank of any system serves as a hub to its economic growth.

Seventh, health sector which is critical to human existence should be given the desired commitment. The mere expression of "commitment and recommitment" by the leaders without practicalities is an albatross to the progress of the continent. Diseases such as Human Immuno Virus (HIV) or Acquired immune Deficiency Syndrome (AIDS), Tuberculosis, Cancer, Maternal and Infant Mortality among other should be given the needed attention so as to salvage the devastating effect they have on the continent. The resolve by the African leaders to dedicate 15% of their various national budgets to health sector should not be reneged. Health personnel in the various member states should be adequately catered for in order to prevent the best brains in the sector from migrating to other continents for greener pasture. This will also prevent unnecessary strikes embarked upon by health workers or medical doctors, which occasion untold consequences on ordinary citizens. Health institutions should be adequately equipped for better services. There should also be seasonal retraining of health workers in other to cope with the emerging challenges.

Eighth, the Peace and Security Council of the African Union should rise up to its responsibilities. The crisis in some member states of the African Union have posed a greater challenge to the continent but if the Peace and Security Council lives up to its expectations, most of the crises witnessed on the continent will be nipped in the bud before they escalate as it happens currently. The Council should make judicious use of its interventionist power to wade into internal crisis in member states so that there will be peace in Africa. The crisis in Sudan, Kenya, Egypt, Benin, Cote d'Ivoire and Libya among others do not portray African Union as an institution that is capable of performing or achieving its set goals. The Peace and Security Council should wake up from its slumber to face the security challenges staring in the face of Africa as a continent.

Ninth, the African Union should be serious with the prosecution of its erring member states' leaders. A situation whereby the Union finds difficulty in taking necessary measures to secure conviction or at least the prosecution of the erring members is appalling and it does not augur well for the Union. The refusal of the Union to prosecute the former President of Chad, Hissane Habre, and the recent refusal to release President Omar Al-Bashir of Sudan for trial by International Criminal Court for crimes against humanity clearly shows that the Union is not honest and serious about the prosecution of erring leaders. It is recommended further that, as contemplated by some member states, if the African Court of Justice and Human Rights comes to operation, its jurisdiction should be expanded in order for it to try crimes against humanity. When this is done, the confidence of the citizenry in the Union will be restored.

Last, the emerging global sophisticated crime of terrorism should be thoroughly checked in order to avert its devastating impact on the continent. Improvement in the area of science and technology will do a great deal in this regard.

We need to remind our brothers in South Africa that people are of two types. They are either your brother and sisters by ethnic affiliation or brothers and sisters by common humanity.

APPENDIX

CONSTITUTIVE ACT OF THE AFRICAN UNION

The Constitutive Act
We, Heads of State and Government of the Member States of the
Organization of African Unity (OAU):
1.   The President of the People's Democratic Republic of Algeria
2.   The President of the Republic of Angola
3.   The President of the Republic of Benin
4.   The President of the Republic of Botswana
5.   The President of Burkina Faso
6.   The President of the Republic of Burundi
7.   The President of the Republic of Cameroon
8.   The President of the Republic of Cape Verde
9.   The President of the Central African Republic
10.   The President of the Republic of Chad
11.   The President of the Islamic Federal Republic of the Comoros
12.   The President of the Republic of the Congo
13.   The President of the Republic of Côte d'Ivoire
14.   The President of the Democratic Republic of Congo
15.   The President of the Republic of Djibouti
16.   The President of the Arab Republic of Egypt
17.   The President of the State of Eritrea
18.   The Prime Minister of the Federal Democratic Republic of
        Ethiopia
19.   The President of the Republic of Equatorial Guinea
20.   The President of the Gabonese Republic
21.   The President of the Republic of The Gambia
22.   The President of the Republic of Ghana
23.   The President of the Republic of Guinea
24.   The President of the Republic of Guinea Bissau
25.   The President of the Republic of Kenya
26.   The Prime Minister of Lesotho
27.   The President of the Republic of Liberia
28.   The Leader of the 1st of September Revolution of

	the Great Socialist People's Libyan Arab Jamahiriya
29.	The President of the Republic of Madagascar
30.	The President of the Republic of Malawi
31.	The President of the Republic of Mali
32.	The President of the Islamic Republic of Mauritania
33.	The Prime Minister of the Republic of Mauritius
34.	The President of the Republic of Mozambique
35.	The President of the Republic of Namibia
36.	The President of the Republic of Niger
37.	The President of the Federal Republic of Nigeria
38.	The President of the Republic of Rwanda
39.	The President of the Sahrawi Arab Democratic Republic
40.	The President of the Republic of Sao Tome and Principe
41.	The President of the Republic of Senegal
42.	The President of the Republic of Seychelles
43.	The President of the Republic of Sierra Leone
44.	The President of the Republic of Somalia
45.	The President of the Republic of South Africa
46.	The President of the Republic of Sudan
47.	The King of Swaziland
48.	The President of the United Republic of Tanzania
49.	The President of the Togolese Republic
50.	The President of the Republic of Tunisia
51.	The President of the Republic of Uganda
52.	The President of the Republic of Zambia
53.	The President of the Republic of Zimbabwe

INSPIRED by the noble ideals which guided the founding fathers of our Continental Organisation and generations of Pan-Africanists in their determination to promote unity, solidarity, cohesion and cooperation among the peoples of Africa and African States;

CONSIDERING the principles and objectives stated in the Charter of the Organisation of African Unity and the Treaty establishing the African Economic Community;

RECALLING the heroic struggles waged by our peoples and our countries for political independence, human dignity and economic emancipation;

CONSIDERING that since its inception, the Organization of African Unity has played a determining and invaluable role in the liberation of the continent, the affirmation of a common identity and the process of attainment of the unity of our continent and has provided a unique framework for our collective action in Africa and in our relations with the rest of the world.

DETERMINED to take up the multifaceted challenges that confront our continent and peoples in the light of the social, economic and political changes taking place in the world;

CONVINCED of the need to accelerate the process of implementing the Treaty establishing the African Economic Community in order to promote the socio-economic development of Africa and to face more effectively the challenges posed by globalization;

GUIDED by our common vision of a united and strong Africa and by the need to build a partnership between governments and all segments of civil society, in particular women, youth and the private sector, in order to strengthen solidarity and cohesion among our peoples;

CONSCIOUS of the fact that the scourge of conflicts in Africa constitutes a major impediment to the socio-economic development of the continent and of the need to promote peace, security and stability as a prerequisite for the implementation of our development and integration agenda;

DETERMINED to promote and protect human and peoples' rights, consolidate democratic institutions and culture, and to ensure good governance and the rule of law;

FURTHER DETERMINED to take all necessary measures to strengthen our common institutions and provide them with the necessary powers and resources to enable them discharge their respective mandates effectively;

RECALLING the Declaration which we adopted at the Fourth Extraordinary Session of our Assembly in Sirte, the Great Socialist People's Libyan Arab Jamahiriya, on 9.9. 99, in which we decided to establish an African Union, in conformity with the ultimate objectives of the

Charter of our Continental Organisation and the Treaty establishing the African Economic Community;

HAVE AGREED AS FOLLOWS:

Article 1
Definitions

In this Constitutive Act:
"Act" means the present Constitutive Act;
"AEC" means the African Economic Community;
"Assembly" means the Assembly of Heads of State and Government of the Union;
"Charter" means the Charter of the OAU;
"Commission" means the Secretariat of the Union;
"Committee" means a Specialized Technical Committee of the Union;
"Council" means the Economic, Social and Cultural Council of the Union;
"Court" means the Court of Justice of the Union;
"Executive Council" means the Executive Council of Ministers of the Union;
"Member State" means a Member State of the Union;
"OAU" means the Organization of African Unity;
"Parliament" means the Pan-African Parliament of the Union;
"Union" means the African Union established by the present Constitutive Act.

Article 2
Establishment
The African Union is hereby established in accordance with the provisions of this Act.

Article 3
Objectives
The objectives of the Union shall be to:
(a)   achieve greater unity and solidarity between the African countries and the peoples of Africa;
(b)   defend the sovereignty, territorial integrity and independence of its Member States;
(c)   accelerate the political and socio-economic integration of the continent;

(d)   promote and defend African common positions on issues of interest to the continent and its peoples;

(e)   encourage international cooperation, taking due account of the Charter of the United Nations and the Universal Declaration of Human Rights;

(f)   promote peace, security, and stability on the continent;

(g)   promote democratic principles and institutions, popular participation and good governance;

(h)   promote and protect human and peoples' rights in accordance with the African Charter on Human and Peoples' Rights and other relevant human rights instruments;

(i)   establish the necessary conditions which enable the continent to play its rightful role in the global economy and in international negotiations;

(j)   promote sustainable development at the economic, social and cultural levels as well as the integration of African economies;

(k)   promote co-operation in all fields of human activity to raise the living standards of African peoples;

(l)   coordinate and harmonize the policies between the existing and future Regional Economic Communities for the gradual attainment of the objectives of the Union;

(m)   advance the development of the continent by promoting research in all fields, in particular, in science and technology

(n)   work with relevant international partners in the eradication of preventable diseases and the promotion of good health on the continent.

Article 4
Principles

The Union shall function in accordance with the following principles:

(a)   sovereign equality and interdependence among Member States of the Union;

(b)   respect of borders existing on achievement of independence;

(c)   participation of the African peoples in the activities of the Union;

(d)   establishment of a common defence policy for the African Continent;

(e)   peaceful resolution of conflicts among Member States of the Union through such appropriate means as may be decided upon by the Assembly;

(f)   prohibition of the use of force or threat to use force among Member States of the Union;

(g)   non-interference by any Member State in the internal affairs of another;

(h)   the right of the Union to intervene in a Member State pursuant to a decision of the Assembly in respect of grave circumstances, namely: war crimes, genocide and crimes against humanity;

(i)   peaceful co-existence of Member States and their right to live in peace and security;

(j)   the right of Member States to request intervention from the Union in order to restore peace and security;

(k)   promotion of self-reliance within the framework of the Union;

(l)   promotion of gender equality;

(m)   respect for democratic principles, human rights, the rule of law and good governance;

(n)   promotion of social justice to ensure balanced economic development;

(o)   respect for the sanctity of human life, condemnation and rejection of impunity and political assassination, acts of terrorism and subversive activities;

(p)   condemnation and rejection of unconstitutional changes of governments.

Article 5
Organs of the Union

1.   The organs of the Union shall be:
    (a)   The Assembly of the Union;
    (b)   The Executive Council;
    (c)   The Pan-African Parliament;
    (d)   The Court of Justice;
    (e)   The Commission;
    (f)   The Permanent Representatives Committee;
    (g)   The Specialised Technical Committees;
    (h)   The Economic, Social and Cultural Council;
    (i)   The Financial Institutions;

2. Other organs that the Assembly may decide to establish.

Article 6
The Assembly

1.   The Assembly shall be composed of Heads of States and Government or their duly accredited representatives.
2.   The Assembly shall be the supreme organ of the Union.
3. The Assembly shall meet at least once a year in ordinary session.
At the request of any Member State and on approval by a two thirds majority of the Member States, the Assembly shall meet in extraordinary session.
4.   The Office of the Chairman of the Assembly shall be for a period of one year by a Head of State or Government elected after consultations among the Member States.

Article 7
Decisions of the Assembly

1.   The Assembly shall take its decisions by consensus or, failing which, by a two-thirds majority of the Member States of the Union.

However, procedural matters, including the question of whether a matter is one of procedure or not, shall be decided by a simple majority.
2.   Two-thirds of the total membership of the Union shall form a quorum at any meeting of the Assembly.

Article 8
Rules of Procedure of the Assembly

The Assembly shall adopt its own Rules of Procedure.

Article 9
Powers and Functions of the Assembly

1.   The functions of the Assembly shall be to:
(a)   determine the common policies of the Union;
(b)   receive, consider and take decisions on reports and recommendations from the other organs of the Union;
(c)   consider requests for Membership of the Union;
(d)   establish any organ of the Union;
(e)   monitor the implementation of policies and decisions of the Union as well ensure compliance by all Member States;
(f)   adopt the budget of the Union;

(g) give directives to the Executive Council on the management of conflicts, war and other emergency situations and the restoration of peace;

(h) appoint and terminate the appointment of the judges of the Court of Justice;

(i) appoint the Chairman of the Commission and his or her deputy or deputies and Commissioners of the Commission and determine their functions and terms of office

2. The Assembly may delegate any of its powers and functions to any organ of the Union.

Article 10
The Executive Council

1. The Executive Council shall be composed of the Ministers of Foreign Affairs or such other Ministers or Authorities as are designated by the Governments of Member States.

2. The Executive Council shall meet at least twice a year in ordinary session. It shall also meet in an extra-ordinary session at the request of any Member State and upon approval by two-thirds of all Member States.

Article 11
Decisions of the Executive Council

1. The Executive Council shall take its decisions by consensus or, failing which, by a two-thirds majority of the Member States. However, procedural matters, including the question of whether a matter is one of procedure or not, shall be decided by a simple majority.

2. Two-thirds of the total membership of the Union shall form a quorum at any meeting of the Executive Council.

Article 12
Rules of Procedure of the Executive Council
The Executive Council shall adopt its own Rules of Procedure.

Article 13
Functions of the Executive Council

1. The Executive Council shall coordinate and take decisions on policies in areas of common interest to the Member States, including the following:

(a)   foreign trade;
(b)   energy, industry and mineral resources;
(c)   food, agricultural and animal resources, livestock production and forestry;
(d)   water resources and irrigation;
(e)   environmental protection, humanitarian action and disaster response and relief;
(f)   transport and communications;
(g)   insurance;
(h)   education, culture, health and human resources development;
(i)   science and technology;
(j)   nationality, residency and immigration matters;
(k)   social security, including the formulation of mother and child care policies, as well as policies relating to the disabled and the handicapped;
(l)   establishment of a system of African awards, medals and prizes.

2.   The Executive Council shall be responsible to the Assembly. It shall consider issues referred to it and monitor the implementation of policies formulated by the Assembly.

3.   The Executive Council may delegate any of its powers and functions mentioned in paragraph 1 of this Article to the Specialized Technical Committees established under Article 14 of this Act.

Article 14
The Specialised Technical Committees Establishment and Composition

1.   There is hereby established the following Specialized Technical Committees, which shall be responsible to the Executive Council:

(a)   The Committee on Rural Economy and Agricultural Matters;
(b)   The Committee on Monetary and Financial Affairs;
(c)   The Committee on Trade, Customs and Immigration Matters;
(d)   The Committee on Industry, Science and Technology, Energy, Natural Resources and Environment;
(e)   The Committee on Transport, Communications and Tourism;
(f)   The Committee on Health, Labour and Social Affairs; and
(g)   The Committee on Education, Culture and Human Resources.

2. The Assembly shall, whenever it deems appropriate, restructure the existing Committees or establish other Committees.
3. The Specialised Technical Committees shall be composed of Ministers or senior officials responsible for sectors falling within their respective areas of competence.

Article 15
Functions of the Specialized Technical Committees

(a) prepare projects and programmes of the Union and submit it to the Executive Council;

(b) ensure the supervision, follow-up and the evaluation of the implementation of decisions taken by the organs of the Union;

(c) ensure the coordination and harmonisation of projects and programmes of the Union;

(d) submit to the Executive Council either on its own initiative or at the request of the Executive Council, reports and recommendations on the implementation of the provisions of this Act; and

(e) carry out any other functions assigned to it for the purpose of ensuring the implementation of the provisions of this Act.

Article 16
Meetings

Subject to any directives given by the Executive Council, each Committee shall meet as often as necessary and shall prepare its Rules of Procedure and submit them to the Executive Council for approval.

Article 17
The Pan-African Parliament

1. In order to ensure the full participation of African peoples in the development and economic integration of the continent, a Pan-African Parliament shall be established.
2. The composition, powers, functions and organization of the Pan-African Parliament shall be defined in a protocol relating thereto.

Article 18
The Court of Justice

1. A Court of Justice of the Union shall be established;
2. The statute, composition and functions of the Court of Justice shall be defined in a protocol relating thereto.

Article 19
The Financial Institutions

The Union shall have the following Financial Institutions whose rules and regulations shall be defined in the protocol relating thereto:

(a)   The African Central Bank;
(b)   The African Monetary Fund;
(c)   The African Investment Bank.

Article 20
The Commission

1.   There shall be established a Commission of the Union, which shall be the Secretariat of the Union.
2.   The Commission shall be composed of the Chairman, his or her deputy or deputies and the Commissioners. They shall be assisted by the necessary staff for the smooth functioning of the Commission.
3.   The structure, functions and regulations of the Commission shall be determined by the Assembly.

Article 21
The Permanent Representatives Committee

1.   There shall be established a Permanent Representatives Committee. It shall be composed of Permanent Representatives to the Union and other Plenipotentiaries of Member States.

2.   The Permanent Representatives Committee shall be charged with the responsibility of preparing the work of the Executive Council and acting on the Executive Council's instructions. It may set up such sub-committees or working groups as it may deem necessary.

Article 22
The Economic, Social and Cultural Council

1.   The Economic, Social and Cultural Council shall be an advisory organ composed of different social and professional groups of the Member States of the Union.
2.   The functions, powers, composition and organization of the Economic, Social and Cultural Council shall be determined by the Assembly.

Article 23
Imposition of Sanctions

1. The Assembly shall determine the appropriate sanctions to be imposed on any Member State that defaults in the payment of its contributions to the budget of the Union in the following manner: denial of the right to speak at meetings, to vote, to present candidates for any position or post within the Union or to benefit from any activity or commitments, therefrom;

2. Furthermore, any Member State that fails to comply with the decisions and policies of the Union may be subjected to other sanctions, such as the denial of transport and communications links with other Member States, and other measures of a political and economic nature to be determined by the Assembly.

Article 24
The Headquarters of the Union

1. The Headquarters of the Union shall be in Addis Ababa in the Federal Democratic Republic of Ethiopia.

2. There may be established such other offices of the Union as the Assembly may, on the recommendation of the Executive Council, determine.

Article 25
Working Languages

The working languages of the Union and all its institutions shall be, if possible, African languages, Arabic, English, French and Portuguese.

Article 26
Interpretations

The Court shall be seized with matters of interpretation arising from the application or implementation of this Act. Pending its establishment, such matters shall be submitted to the Assembly of the Union, which shall decide by a two-thirds majority.

Article 27
Signature, Ratification and Accession

1. This action shall open to signature, ratification and accession by the Member States of the OAU in accordance with their respective constitutional procedures.

2. The instruments of ratification shall be deposited with the Sec-
    retary-General of the OAU.

3. Any Member State of the OAU acceding to this Act after its
    entry into force shall deposit the instrument of accession with
    the Chairman of the Commission.

Article 28
Entry into Force

This Act shall enter into force thirty (30) days after the deposit of the
instruments of ratification by two-thirds of the Member States of the
OAU.

Article 29
Admission to Membership

1. Any African State may, at any time after the entry into force of
    this Act, notify the Chairman of the Commission of its inten-
    tion to accede to this Act and to be admitted as a member of
    the Union.

2. The Chairman of the Commission shall, upon receipt of such
    notification, transmit copies thereof to all Member States. Ad-
    mission shall be decided by a simple majority of the Member
    States. The decision of each Member State shall be transmitted
    to the Chairman of the Commission who shall, upon receipt of
    the required number of votes, communicate the decision to the
    State concerned.

Article 30
Suspension

Governments which shall come to power through unconstitutional
means shall not be allowed to participate in the activities of the Union.

Article 31
Cessation of Membership

1. Any State which desires to renounce its membership shall for-
    ward a written notification to the Chairman of Commission,
    who shall inform Member States thereof. At the end of one
    year from the date of such notification, if not withdrawn, the
    Act shall cease to apply with respect to the renouncing State,
    which shall thereby cease to belong to the Union.

2. During the period of one year referred to in paragraph 1 of this
    Article, any Member State wishing to withdraw from the Union

shall comply with the provisions of this Act and shall be bound to discharge its obligations under this Act up to the date of its withdrawal.

Article 32
Amendment and Revision

1. Any Member State may submit proposals for the amendment or revision of this Act.

2. Proposals for amendment or revision shall be submitted to the Chairman of the Commission who shall transmit same to Member States within thirty (30) days of receipt thereof.

3. The Assembly, upon the advice of the Executive Council, shall examine these proposals within a period of one year following notification of Member States, in accordance with the provisions of paragraph 2 of this Article;

4. Amendments or revisions shall be adopted by the Assembly by consensus or, failing which, by a two-thirds majority and submitted for ratification by all Member States in accordance with their respective constitutional procedures. They shall enter into force thirty (30) days after the deposit of the instruments of ratification with the Chairman of the Commission by a two-thirds majority of the Member States.

Article 33
Transitional Arrangements and Final Provisions

1. This Act shall replace the Charter of the Organisation of African Unity. However, the Charter shall remain operative for a transitional period of one year or such further period as may be determined by the Assembly, following the entry into force of the Act, for the purpose of enabling the OAU/AEC to undertake the necessary measures regarding the devolution of its assets and liabilities to the Union and all matters relating thereto.

2. The provisions of this Act shall take precedence over and supersede any inconsistent or contrary provisions of the Treaty establishing the African Economic Community.

3. Upon the entry into force of this Act, all necessary measures shall be undertaken to implement its provisions and to ensure the establishment of the organs provided for under the Act in accordance with any directives or decisions which may be

    adopted in this regard by the Parties thereto within the transitional period stipulated above.

4.   Pending the establishment of the Commission, the OAU General Secretariat shall be the interim Secretariat of the Union.

5.   This Act, drawn up in four (4) original texts in the Arabic, English, French and Portuguese languages, all four (4) being equally authentic, shall be deposited with the Secretary-General of the OAU and, after its entry into force, with the Chairman of the Commission who shall transmit a certified true copy of the Act to the Government of each signatory State. The Secretary-General of the OAU and the Chairman of the Commission shall notify all signatory States of the dates of the deposit of the instruments of ratification or accession and shall upon entry into force of the Act register the same with the Secretariat of the United Nations.

IN WITNESS WHEREOF, WE have adopted this Act.
Done at Lome, Togo, this 11th day of July, 2000.

ABBREVIATIONS

AU ....African Union
OAU ....Organisation of African Unity
IDP ....Internally Displaced Person
E.U. ....European Union
ECOWAS .... Economic Community of West African States
PALU ....Pan-African Lawyers Union
OATU ....Organisation of African Trade Union
PAEF ....Pan-African Employers Federation
PAWO ....Pan-African Women Organisation
ECOSOCC ....Economic, Social and Cultural Council
CSO ....Civil Society Organisation
NEPAD ....New Partnership for African Development
PAIDF........................Pan-African Infrastructure Development Fund
CAADP....Comprehensive Africa Agricultural Development Programme
ADC...Industrial Development Corporation
PIDA......................Programme Infrastructure Development in Africa
ICF..Investment Climate Facility
UN..United nations
HSGIC.....Heads of State and Government Implementation Committee
PSC..Peace and Security Council

CASES

www.ingramcontent.com/pod-product-compliance
Lightning Source LLC
Chambersburg PA
CBHW070903270326
41927CB00011B/2446